In *Results Now 2.0*, **Mike Schmoker ho.... ...** education—a mirror that is brutally honest and whose reflection a lot of people won't like to see. Which is exactly the point. One of the key features of our education system is something Schmoker calls *the buffer*: a barrier that prevents us from reckoning with the realities of schooling; it allows us to shut down conversations that challenge the **defunct ideas that pervade everyday practice and fill the syllabi at schools of education**. In short, it exacerbates the staggering gap between what we do and what students need. This book will lay that gap bare—while it illuminates **the immense opportunity to make dramatic improvements to schooling.**

—Doug Lemov
author of *Teach Like a Champion 3.0*

Spurning fads and buzzwords du jour, Mike Schmoker offers an **update to his wildly popular** *Results Now,* **an update chock-full of sound advice** backed by years of solid research. **A must-read for any educator** seeking to improve how we educate our next generation of voters.

—Sam Wineburg
Margaret Jacks Professor of Education, Stanford University

Schmoker is a superb writer: With many well-aimed hammer blows, **he pulverizes the notion that the most effective practices are being implemented in our school systems**. I thought "checking for understanding" and the sharp focus on reading and writing I was seeing in some charter schools was spreading steadily throughout the country. His excellent book suggests otherwise. And the education schools appear to still not be helping new teachers master the most fundamental practices. Read this book but prepare to be upset.

—Jay Mathews
author and education columnist, *The Washington Post*

Mike Schmoker has issued an urgent call to action and **challenges educators to acknowledge "the facts" and address shortcomings in the system NOW**, before another generation is sacrificed on the altar of the status quo.

—Carol Jago
author, teacher, and former president of the
National Council of Teachers of English

Imagine **a book that fearlessly turns over the rocks** to expose what isn't working in schools today—floundering teams; feckless group work; the mirage of instructional supervision; being clueless in academe; ineffective professional development; and the whims, fads, opportunism, and ideology that run rampant. Schmoker is angry—we know what to do, but we do anything but—and **he offers excellent ways out of this smog and delusion**.

—**John Hattie**
laureate professor, Melbourne Graduate School of Education;
author of *Visible Learning*

This **powerful book embodies a can-do attitude and shows educators how to help their students achieve at remarkably high levels.** But don't expect happy talk. Schmoker is clear-eyed about the "brutal facts" of our education system's failures and what it will take to overcome them. Don't open this volume unless you are ready to *change.*

—**Michael J. Petrilli**
president, Thomas B. Fordham Institute

In this profoundly important book, Mike Schmoker challenges parents, teachers, educational leaders, and policymakers to compare our perceptions with reality. **Too many schools persist in mysticism rather than evidence-based practices.** The fundamental challenge is not that we fail to understand how to provide effective curriculum, instruction, and leadership but rather that our institutions are reluctant to translate evidence into action. Schmoker will not allow the reader to compromise. Either we follow the difficult scholar's path to excellence and challenge or descend onto the easier path of popularity and indolence. **This is a book not merely to read but to be studied, debated, and shared with communities of teachers, parents, leaders, and policymakers.** Let us listen to Schmoker.

—**Douglas Reeves**
author of *Fearless Schools*

Mike Schmoker reminds us that an engaging, **cohesive, thinking-rich curriculum**—ideally refined by teachers working collaboratively—can provide a corrective to the plethora of disjointed "programs" school districts often impose upon schools. **Thanks again for the heads-up, Mike!**

—**Lisa Delpit**
award-winning author of *Teaching When the World Is On Fire*
and *Multiplication Is for White People*

In *Results Now 2.0*, Mike Schmoker takes on a "brutal fact": that despite good intentions, **American schools are *preventing* students from receiving a rich, literate education**. More importantly, this book **lays out specific, doable steps** regarding curriculum, instruction, and professional development—**steps that lead to immediate and profound improvement.** In a time of "so much reform and so little change," this book should be read by policymakers, board members, superintendents, curriculum supervisors, staff developers, department chairs, and teachers—in short, by anyone interested in improving schools.

—**Kelly Gallagher**
educator and author of *Readicide*

In this important and timely book, Mike Schmoker explains that **without the right tools, PLC teams "flounder without knowing why."** Schmoker then describes those tools—the specific curriculum, literacy, and pedagogical practices **that enable effective teams to get amazing results with their students**.

—**Kim Marshall**
author, educator, and editor of *The Marshall Memo*

In this **timely and engaging book**, Mike Schmoker cuts through what he calls "the buffer"—a smokescreen of mistaken assumptions—to reveal **painful truths about American schools**. He confronts us with evidence that, for example, students often get coloring projects instead of rigorous reading and writing assignments, even at upper grade levels. But he also offers practical, realistic **strategies that can yield dramatic improvements**.

—**Natalie Wexler**
author of *The Knowledge Gap*

Phenomenal. **Schmoker is brutally honest** here about the current state of education in the United States **while being equally hopeful** about what can and needs to be done about it. For us educators who are tired of excuses and subpar outcomes for kids, who are looking to drive true change, **Schmoker has given us our road map.**

—**Michael Sonbert**
founder, Skyrocket Education

RESULTS NOW 2.0

ASCD MEMBER BOOK

Many ASCD members received this book as a
member benefit upon its initial release.

Learn more at: **www.ascd.org/memberbooks**

Other ASCD books by Mike Schmoker:

*Focus: Elevating the Essentials to Radically
Improve Student Learning, 2nd Edition*

*Leading with Focus: Elevating the Essentials
for School and District Improvement*

*Results: The Key to Continuous
School Improvement, 2nd Edition*

*The Results Fieldbook: Practical Strategies
from Dramatically Improved Schools*

RESULTS NOW 2.0

The Untapped Opportunities
for Swift, Dramatic Gains
in Achievement

MIKE SCHMOKER

Arlington, Virginia USA

2800 Shirlington Rd., Suite 1001 • Arlington, VA 22206 USA
Phone: 800-933-2723 or 703-578-9600 • Fax: 703-575-5400
Website: www.ascd.org • Email: member@ascd.org
Author guidelines: www.ascd.org/write

Penny Reinart, *Deputy Executive Director;* Genny Ostertag, *Managing Director, Book Acquisitions and Editing;* Bill Varner, *Senior Acquisitions Editor;* Mary Beth Nielsen, *Director, Book Editing;* Jamie Greene, *Senior Editor;* Thomas Lytle, *Creative Director;* Donald Ely, *Art Director;* MaameYaa Danso/The Hatcher Group, *Graphic Designer;* Kelly Marshall, *Production Manager;* Christopher Logan, *Senior Production Specialist;* Cynthia Stock, *Typesetter;* Shajuan Martin, *E-Publishing Specialist*

All web links in this book are correct as of the publication date below but may have become inactive or otherwise modified since that time. If you notice a deactivated or changed link, please email books@ascd.org with the words "Link Update" in the subject line. In your message, please specify the web link, the book title, and the page number on which the link appears.

PAPERBACK ISBN: 978-1-4166-3199-6   ASCD product #123048
PDF EBOOK ISBN: 978-1-4166-3200-9; see Books in Print for other formats.
Quantity discounts are available: email programteam@ascd.org or call 800-933-2723, ext. 5773, or 703-575-5773. For desk copies, go to www.ascd.org/deskcopy.

ASCD Member Book No. FY23-7 (May 2023 P). ASCD Member Books mail to Premium (P), Select (S), and Institutional Plus (I+) members on this schedule: Jan, PSI+; Feb, P; Apr, PSI+; May, P; Jul, PSI+; Aug, P; Sep, PSI+; Nov, PSI+; Dec, P. For current details on membership, see www.ascd.org/membership.

Library of Congress Cataloging-in-Publication Data

Names: Schmoker, Michael J., author.
Title: Results now 2.0 : the untapped opportunities for swift, dramatic
   gains in achievement / Mike Schmoker.
Description: Arlington, VA : ASCD, 2023. | Includes bibliographical
   references and index.
Identifiers: LCCN 2022059240 (print) | LCCN 2022059241 (ebook) | ISBN
   9781416631996 (paperback) | ISBN 9781416632009 (pdf)
Subjects: LCSH: School improvement programs—United States. | Educational
   change—United States. | Education—Aims and objectives—United States.
Classification: LCC LB2822.82 .S357 2023 (print) | LCC LB2822.82 (ebook)
   | DDC 370.973--dc23/eng/20230113
LC record available at https://lccn.loc.gov/2022059240
LC ebook record available at https://lccn.loc.gov/2022059241

30 29 28 27 26 25 24 23   1 2 3 4 5 6 7 8 9 10 11 12

For Richard F. Elmore
(1953–2021)

"The opportunity is, for us as a field, to finish what we started, for us to usher in a Golden Age of Educational Practice."

—Michael Petrilli, Fordham Institute

"Leadership is about . . . creating a climate where the truth is heard and the brutal facts confronted."

—Jim Collins, Good to Great

"Improvement takes recognition of and moral outrage at ineffective practices."

—Roland Barth, Harvard Graduate School of Education

"Education remains the civil rights issue of our time."

—John King, The Education Trust

RESULTS NOW 2.0

Preface

The primary purpose of this book, like that of its first edition, is to demonstrate the opportunity for dramatic school improvement by juxtaposing the most effective educational practices with the more common but inferior practices that prevail in most schools. As with its predecessor, I will advocate for having teachers work in instructionally focused teams as members of true professional learning communities, which were given prominence by the late Rick and Becky DuFour.

But my center of gravity has shifted. I've discovered that collaborative teams are more effective when their work is informed by the three core elements I describe in Chapters 2 through 4—namely, curriculum, literacy, and effective instruction. In the absence of a focus on these fundamental practices, teams flounder without knowing why. Since the first edition of this book, which appeared in 2006, the gap between these essential practices and classroom actualities has grown wider. It's even more urgent now to address this gap in light of plummeting achievement levels that resulted from disruptions to schooling related to the COVID-19 pandemic.

This book features a number of exceptionally successful schools that demonstrate the power of these three core elements, but be forewarned: it will also contain many brutal facts. That's because only a close encounter with education's most egregious failings can reveal its richest, most readily available solutions. As Jim Collins (2001) writes, the price of substantial progress is a willingness to "turn over rocks ... even if what you see can scare the hell out of you" (p. 72).

We will turn over many rocks in these pages because what's beneath them directs us to straightforward solutions that can produce the best schools we've ever had.

Finally, some of the very best studies I cite are not as recent as others. Don't dismiss them: their findings, from all I read and observe, accurately represent the existing state of education for which no contradictory evidence has emerged.

Introduction:
Golden Prospects—
And Precedents

Education isn't just another issue. It is the most powerful force for accelerating economic growth, reducing poverty, and lifting middle-class living standards. Well-educated adults earn much more, live longer, and are happier than poorly educated adults.

—David Leonhardt, senior writer, *The New York Times*

Carefully read David Leonhardt's quotation above. He's referring to a prestigious study that reveals the immeasurable, lifelong benefits of a high-quality education (Greenstone et al., 2012). Unfortunately, our current K–12 educational system prevents most students from receiving such an education. That's because it operates, at every level, in defiance of logic and evidence. And that's precisely why our schools could be on the precipice of a "golden age" (Petrilli, 2014). The system's most egregious deficiencies are eminently fixable. Moreover, the transformation of our schools can start with the simplest of small steps.

The chief hindrance to historic improvements may well be this: the most prodigious opportunities hide from us; the "superstructure of schooling" has become highly adept at concealing its gravest defects and its failure to act in accordance with its hard-earned research base

1

(Elmore, 2000, p. 6). To break through, we have to stare down the gap between proven practice and common practice.

That encounter will reveal a rich vein of opportunity that will enable us to turn from counterproductive methods and routines to the powerful, evidence-based actions I describe in the chapters that follow. As we'll see, scholars use words like *miraculous, stunningly powerful,* and *whopping* to describe their effect. In those rare schools where educators have engaged in those practices, they usually transform schooling within one or two academic years. I'll be citing many such schools, especially in Chapters 2–4.

I wrote this book for those who can't rid themselves of the suspicion that schooling could be profoundly better—right now—if we would only act on the best available research. I wrote it for those who are frustrated by the many indefensible practices that prevail in most schools. And I wrote it for those who believe we could achieve the dream we anticipated at the beginning of the school reform era, when hope for serious, large-scale school improvement ran high.

Such improvement, though, must begin with a kind of shock. As Jim Collins (2001) wrote in *Good to Great*, organizations don't improve unless they "confront the brutal facts" about their shortcomings. Schools must confront the fact that the most dominant school practices today diverge radically from the most amply substantiated methods.

This is not an eccentric view; it's the opinion of widely respected observers of public education. Their work points to the prospect of swift, comprehensive school improvement.

The State of the System

Imagine a profession with the following deficiencies.

- The initial preparation and workplace training of its managers and frontline employees are widely regarded as misguided, if not abysmal.
- Consequently, malpractice is not occasional but *predominant* because the most effective practices are rarely learned and seldom implemented.

- The daily work of practitioners is virtually unsupervised, and employees work in isolation from one another and with little or no meaningful guidance from leaders or managers.

As I'll demonstrate, this is the current state of education according to every credible study. Nevertheless, it's *precisely such facts that make education ripe for exceptional growth.* What would happen to education if we meaningfully addressed *any one* of these problems? Would we not begin to move the needle toward significantly better schooling? A mountain of research and numerous schools, such as the ones described in this book, point to this prospect.

Can the Truth Set Us Free?

Yes. There are precedents.

A turning point occurred in medicine early in the 20th century. At that time, the most essential, science-based medical practices were routinely ignored in hospitals and training institutions. There were countless cases of unnecessary illness and death. Until, that is, Abraham Flexner was commissioned to study hospitals and medical schools. His frank report shook the world of medical training and practice. Flexner was "not a man to mince words," deeming most of what he saw as "utterly hopeless"; his report "did not merely make waves ... it produced a tsunami of improvements" and transformed medicine forever (Clarfield, 2004, p. 1). Since 1910, his work has saved an incalculable number of lives.

The most widely respected experts are equally scathing in their appraisal of the current state of education in the United States. Their findings will shock many readers. I share them in the hope they will provoke a similar awakening among educators and the public, an awakening that could well lead to a "tsunami of improvements" in schooling.

As in the field of medicine, the key is to disrupt complacency by providing a less airbrushed picture of K–12 schooling to the widest possible audience of education's stakeholders. Only this can create an urgency for serious action.

There is promising news on this front from a study sponsored by several prominent foundations: UnidosUS, Univision, the National PTA, and the National Urban League (Carnegie Corporation of New York, 2018). The researchers found that accurate information radically alters people's sunny perceptions of school quality. For instance, parents have long given high marks to the schools their children attend and feel minimal urgency to improve them. About 90 percent believe their children are performing "at or above grade level." This is a gross misperception since current schooling practices guarantee that *fewer than one in three students* performs at grade level in reading and math (Burnette II, 2018).

When this incongruity is shared with parents, their positive school perceptions plummet. The funders of this study believe, as I do, that this epiphany is the crucial first step toward improvement. It was the first step for medicine and for all of the organizations Collins describes in *Good to Great.*

Of course, awareness isn't enough; it must lead to the discovery of *why* students perform poorly. There's no mystery here. As Rick Hess and Mike Goldstein (2022) write for *Education Week,* "The truth is that schools have long employed practices with scant empirical grounding" (p. 1). This is the most brutal, overarching fact of all—that in the overwhelming majority of schools, inferior, unproven methods currently supplant the most powerful, empirically proven practices. If implemented, those proven practices would result in unprecedented improvements in our schools and classrooms—beyond any doubt. But this can't happen until educators and the public perceive the yawning gap between common practice and evidence-based practice—and the dire consequences of that gap.

From Information to Transformation

As the Flexner report's effect on medicine illustrates, an encounter with the right facts can create moral urgency and lead to dramatic progress. Such encounters have led to stunning improvements in business, medicine, education, and athletics (Collins, 2001; Schmoker, 2018). In each sphere, improvements were immediate and dramatic.

For example, consider the state of high jumping before the adoption of the technique known as the Fosbury Flop. It was resisted until coaches saw its impact at track meets, and then it became impossible to ignore the evidence that the "flop" gave almost any high jumper a large, almost overnight advantage (Burnton, 2012).

Or consider the success rate of organ transplants once doctors prescribed a drug regimen that prevents the body from rejecting donor organs. It made it possible for me to donate a kidney to my sister despite my being a poor genetic match. Immunosuppressant drugs have given additional years of life and health to hundreds of thousands of organ recipients.

Or look at medical practice before the routine use of checklists. Doctors were initially resistant to using checklists until they were confronted with the brutal facts—data revealing the consequences of failing to implement well-known, life-saving procedures. In one hospital network alone, checklists saved an estimated 12,000 lives in an *18-month span* by ensuring, for instance, that doctors *washed their hands before surgery* (Heath & Heath, 2011).

Such cases relate directly to education. As educational researchers Daniel Willingham and Andrew Rotherham (2020) write, "In education . . . we still don't wash our hands." In other words, we still fail to implement the most basic, high-impact, thoroughly proven strategies in our schools. As we'll see, teachers are hardly given the chance to do so. That's because they work in a system that substitutes "exuberance for evidence" (Willingham & Rotherham, 2020, para. 7).

Please remember throughout these pages that the opportunity is proportional to the problems we expose. When we identify and then replace typical practices with superior ones, schools don't just improve; they improve dramatically and often with amazing speed (Marshall, 2003).

This fact is worth underlining: the most effective but neglected methods work fast, with gains all but guaranteed within a single school year (Joyce, Wolf, & Calhoun, 1993; Wiliam, 2007). Every school cited in this book began to see classroom progress within weeks and made substantial achievement gains in one or two years.

Such claims may sound extravagant. I'm not alone in making them.

A Golden Age—Really?

Some of the most internationally respected voices in education have made bold claims about the effect of shifting from common practices to the best proven ones. Prominent educational researcher Robert Marzano (2003) has written that a shift to evidence-based practices would lead to "an era of unprecedented effectiveness" (p. 10). He cites hundreds of studies to substantiate this claim. He calculates that two to three times as many students will succeed on daily lessons when we begin to implement such methods.

Doug Lemov (2015) shared that intensive training in effective practices would enable us to achieve a "massive breakthrough in teacher quality and achievement" (personal communication). John Hattie (2009) amassed and analyzed thousands of educational studies, involving millions of students in several nations. His research revealed that certain strategies are *several times* as effective as those we typically see in classrooms. Renowned researcher Michael Fullan (2010) has pointed out that implementing the best research-based practices wouldn't just move the needle; it would result in "stunningly powerful consequences" for student learning.

Researchers Peter Mortimore and Pam Sammons (1987) found that the most potent (but largely neglected) teaching strategies have 6 to 10 times as much impact *as all other factors combined*. Linda Darling-Hammond (2010–2011), an advisor to U.S. presidents, cites evidence that a coherent curriculum (the subject of Chapter 2) would account for "soaring" improvements in learning. The impact could erase learning gaps among entering kindergartners that most children never overcome.

Charles Payne (2007) studied instruction in urban schools. He discovered that just one crucial practice (which we look at in Chapter 4) would result in "whopping improvements" (p. 95) among our neediest students. Dylan Wiliam (2007) calculates that the use of that same method would vault U.S. achievement in math from 18th to among the top five countries in international rankings.

William Sanders and Sandra Horn's meta-analyses (1994) demonstrate that *just three years* of effective, evidence-based teaching will result in an improvement of 35 to 50 percentile points in student achievement. That much growth would eliminate most of the existing achievement gaps between high- and lower-achieving subgroups (Bracey, 2004; Marzano, 2007).

Finally, Harvard professor Thomas Kane has done research demonstrating that the best proven strategies could ensure the average classroom would achieve at the same level as the top 25 percent of our classrooms (personal communication, 2022). He estimates that we could close the gap between the United States and the highest achieving countries in the world—in two years.

Two years.

You get the idea. Most importantly, all these researchers lament the manifest absence of proven practices in our schools.

In light of this, is it unreasonable to entertain the possibility of exceptional learning gains in the coming years? Michael Petrilli (2014) is president of the Thomas B. Fordham Institute. He believes we could be on the cusp of a golden age of educational practice if we so wished, but that to enter it, we must repair an educational system that, according to researcher Eric Kalenze (2014), is "upside down."

From Upside Down to Right Side Up

Years before Kalenze wrote those words, Michael Fullan and Michael Barber lamented the "the awful inertia of past decades"—the unchecked accretion of unproven, indefensible practices in our schools (Barber & Fullan, 2005, para. 7). This may sound grim, but these deficiencies only reveal the magnitude of the opportunity for any school or district that decides to turn its efforts "right side up."

Consider an 8th grade team I knew personally, which I'll revisit in subsequent chapters. Midyear, they revised their curriculum and teaching around the principles described in Chapters 2, 3, and 4. Their daily and weekly results improved substantially; after just one semester, their students vaulted from average performance on the state's English language arts assessment to first place. *Exceedingly few schools* employ the practices that worked so well for these teachers and their students. Throughout these chapters, I'll cite numerous teachers, schools, and districts whose success, in only one or two years, was a result of exchanging common but misguided methods for proven elements and strategies.

The Layout of This Book

In **Chapter 1,** we'll consider *the buffer*, which is the major barrier to improvement in the K–12 system, inclusive of university teacher preparation. It conceals our shortcomings (sometimes deliberately) and thus prevents us from ever addressing them. The buffer will be a recurrent theme in these pages.

In **Chapters 2, 3, and 4,** we'll clarify the three most fundamental, evidence-based elements of effective education: curriculum, literacy, and effective instruction. We'll examine the evidence that argues for their primacy and (importantly) the disconcerting gap between these elements and schooling as usual. At the end of each chapter, we'll look at real schools and districts that demonstrate the substantial progress schools can achieve by implementing these evidence-based elements.

In **Chapter 5,** we'll take a deeper look at the buffer—at the specious ideas, illusions, and initiatives that subvert best practices from operating in our schools—and at the consequences of failing to implement those best practices.

In **Chapters 6 and 7,** we'll look at the root causes of our underperforming system: inadequate, misguided teacher preparation and professional development. These continue to impede the adoption of evidence-based practices and the professionalization of the education field.

Finally, in **Chapter 8,** I'll suggest how universities, school districts, and government agencies can turn our deficiencies into immediate, concrete improvements—a golden opportunity for better schools. I'll make the case for what I believe could be the small-scale key to achieving large-scale improvement: the celebration of successful individual lessons implemented by individual teachers or teams. In the end, these are the coins of the realm. They reveal the power of and sustain the focus on the most powerful, evidence-based practices.

Most significantly, at the end of Chapters 2–7, I include a "how-to" section for school leaders. Most of them have never been adequately trained to oversee what teachers are actually teaching in their schools—or how well. The reflection questions listed at the end of these chapters suggest concrete steps leaders can take that will lead to serious improvements in schooling.

Let's now turn to two questions I'm regularly asked:

- Why are the *most effective practices* so rarely employed?
- Why are some of the *least effective practices* so pervasive?

The best explanation can be found in what the late Richard Elmore (1999–2000) called *the buffer.* The buffer hides the richest opportunities for improvement from parents, community members, and board members—and from K–12 educators themselves.

1

The Buffer: The "Brutal Facts" of K–12 Education

We have operated under the BIG LIE for too long.

—Loren Penman, Pennsylvania school administrator

Arne Duncan, the former secretary of education under President Barack Obama, was once asked to tutor a high school junior. Calvin was a solid *B* student, but Duncan was shocked to discover that he could only read at the 2nd grade level. "Our educational system," Duncan realized, "is built on lies" (Riley, 2018, p. A13). Educator and author Doug Lemov had an almost identical experience tutoring a high school athlete who could barely decode text (Green, 2014).

These students were victims of a school system that misrepresents its accomplishments, conceals its failures, and thus deprives millions of students of the ability to read—which is to deny them an education. This is perhaps the most consequential but least known fact about modern schooling: how little students read, or are given the opportunity to read, during the school day. They do lots of other things, as we'll see, but they rarely engage in what is arguably the single most educative activity—reading.

Stories such as Duncan's and Lemov's confirm the work of the late Richard Elmore, to whom this book is dedicated. Elmore employed a profoundly helpful metaphor that I will refer to throughout this book: "the buffer"—that is, the barrier between schooling and its primary stakeholders. The buffer discourages, even punishes, constructive scrutiny of curriculum, instruction, and school leadership. It hides the ground-level workings of schooling "from outside inspection, interference, or disruption" (Elmore, 1999–2000, p. 6).

The buffer makes serious improvement impossible. You can't fight what you don't know or fully grasp. For schools to improve, the right people must be allowed to examine the actual (if unpleasant) workings of the current system, from university education departments to the classroom. Let's now look at some of Elmore's more provocative observations, beginning with his startling findings about instructional oversight.

An Unmanaged System

Elmore was not a voice from the fringe. He was a longtime professor in the Harvard Graduate School of Education and a deeply beloved icon in the field of education (Hess, 2021a). It should concern us that someone of his stature found that "administrators do not manage instruction. . . . [They only] give the impression that they are managing it" (Elmore, 1999–2000, p. 2).

The following quotes are from Elmore's (1999–2000) article in *The American Educator*:

- Despite the appearance of instructional supervision, school leaders do not "manage the way [the school's] basic functions are carried out. . . . Administrators have little to do with decisions about what should be taught . . . how it should be taught, what students should be expected to learn [or] how their learning should be evaluated."
- Teachers work "with little guidance or support" and without the benefit of the most essential research or meaningful training.

- School administration "exists primarily to 'buffer' the instructional core, not to disturb it and certainly not to improve it."
- Although schools "are almost always aboil with some kind of 'change,' they are rarely involved in any deliberate process of improvement."
- Although well-meant, improvement initiatives are mostly intended to promote the "logic of confidence"—that is, to convince parents and the public that "good things are happening in their schools"—so they will not demand changes to how schools are run.
- Attempts at "innovation" are "decidedly not about improving the conditions of teaching and learning for actual teachers and students." (pp. 2–3)

Instructional supervision simply isn't a priority for school leaders. As Elmore once told an interviewer, "There are only a handful of principals who feel like their work has anything to do with instructional practice.... They are not good at it ... that's not what they have gotten rewarded for." In sum, this failure to manage instruction explains why successful instructional practices that grow out of research or exemplary practice "never take root" in more than a few classrooms and schools (Blanding, 2009, para. 2).

We'll be exploring other reasons and root causes for mediocre schooling, but if Elmore's observations are roughly on target, we need not wonder why hundreds of billions of improvement dollars haven't moved the needle on school performance. No profession improves in the absence of effective management. Curriculum and instruction, the soul of schooling, are typically left to teachers "working in isolated classrooms," with little or no support or guidance in proven practices (Elmore, 1999–2000, p. 2).

These are sobering words. Elmore was a spokesperson for those like myself who know that schools will make rapid, dramatic strides once they acknowledge and address their gravest shortcomings. He was not alone.

The Buffer: Past and Present

UCLA's John Goodlad was a revered education professor and a pioneer in school reform. His landmark study (Goodlad et al., 1970) revealed that the majority of what happens in schools is frightfully inappropriate but remains hidden "behind the classroom door." This is especially true in the crucial area of literacy.

Years later, Paul Black and Dylan Wiliam (1998) wrote one of the most widely read educational articles ever published: "Inside the Black Box." They similarly lamented that the actualities of schooling and the richest opportunities for improvement are carefully kept out of sight, within schooling's "black box." Almost 20 years later, the Fordham Institute's Chester Finn (2017) wrote, "When that classroom door closes, [the teacher] can teach pretty much whatever they want, using pretty much whatever materials they want" (p. 1).

Judith Little and colleagues (Little et al., 2003) point out that this insularity reflects a culture that prizes "noninterference" and "privacy," of letting practitioners do "whatever they want" in the service of "harmony." That harmony has a steep cost: it creates a wide berth for malpractice and excuses school administration from ever taking on "the tough work of school improvement" (p. 190).

According to the American Enterprise Institute's Robert Pondiscio (2019), this ethos of noninterference ensures that classroom practice tends to run less on research and empirical evidence than on some combination of philosophy, faith, or personal preference—and that results in the worst imaginable scenario if we care about high-quality education. As Odden and Kelley (2002) point out, effective teaching is quite different from the teaching that typically occurs in most classrooms. This is the predictable result of a system in which isolated, poorly prepared teachers are made to work in the virtual absence of instructional management.

No one seriously disputes these findings. As we'll see in subsequent chapters, a legion of researchers has attempted to shine a light on the difference between perception and reality in schooling. Every now and then, a member of the public gets a glimpse of the peculiar practices that occur inside that "black box." One school board member in Illinois vented his outrage at a public meeting, asking the administration why his daughter had watched 20 movies in a single school year (Harrison, 2010).

The average person would be shocked to know that the school day is filled with time-killing, nonacademic activities—such as watching entire recent-release movies for days in a row, with no clear academic purpose. Should parents and community members be apprised of how common these patterns are in their children's schools? Greater transparency would curb the worst of such practices.

We've been looking at general critiques of schooling. Let's now consider specific aspects that hide from public, parental, and administrative view—from "outside inspection" and intervention. I'll start by describing a typical classroom tour; I've done such tours for decades. In almost all of them, you'll see the same patterns.

A Typical Tour in a "High-Achieving" District

I'm walking through classrooms with the superintendent and assistant superintendent of curriculum and instruction of a highly regarded suburban school district in the U.S. Southwest. It has a large complement of affluent students and *A+* schools.

Despite its glowing reputation, instruction in every school is mostly poor—and remarkably similar to what I see in the lowest-achieving, least advantaged schools I visit.

Before these tours, I always review just a few vital practices that most educators agree are important. We would expect, for instance, to see lessons that appear to derive from a legitimate curriculum. Likewise, we might expect to see instructors employing certain fundamental teaching strategies, such as engaging in ongoing attempts to see if students are keeping up as the lesson progresses (that is, checking for understanding). Then I gently warn my companions that their expectations will probably not be met.

Sure enough, by the fourth or fifth classroom visit, it becomes apparent that many teachers are working from their own private collection of (often dubious) activities and worksheets. We see surprisingly little actual teaching going on; most of the work is being done in unsupervised groups, as students chat quietly. We rarely witness students engaged in purposeful reading, meaningful discussion, or writing—even in English or social studies courses, where those activities should predominate. And we almost never witness students being taught to write effectively.

The instruction we *do* see lacks the widely agreed-on elements of sound, step-by-step teaching, where the teacher clarifies the purpose of the lesson and then alternates among teaching, monitoring student progress, and reteaching as needed (some amount of which is *always* needed in every lesson). We can't help but notice one of the most common forms of malpractice: teachers calling exclusively on the more capable, attentive students who *raise their hands* while the majority sit passively, visibly disengaged. If there is a discussion, it's brief, superficial, and dominated by the hand raisers. The questions asked are seldom probing or analytic; they're mostly regurgative. Finally, watching movies seems to be a feature in a surprising proportion of darkened classrooms, with teachers seldom giving students any legitimate academic purpose for viewing them.

The point of putting such brutal facts on display is this: Every one of these deficiencies would be eliminated the moment we identify the best evidence-based practices, train our teachers to apply them, and monitor their implementation. Until we do this, malpractice will dominate unabated. It will negatively affect almost all K–12 students.

Who's Cheated? Everyone

I assure you that this school district is representative of almost all districts and that this classroom tour is typical of those I've conducted with school administrators in every kind of school in dozens of states. The patterns hide quite effectively behind the buffer, within the "black box."

We need to realize that *all students* are underserved by these patterns, as were my own daughters who were both good students. To some degree, the brightest ones and those from affluent, educated households manage to survive these deficiencies. Those students benefit from advanced coursework in high school and are more apt to receive grade-appropriate materials to learn from (Kane & Steiner, 2019).

Nevertheless, even our best students are cheated. Their intellectual and expressive capacities have been stymied for decades, with the highest cohort realizing the greatest decline. Among the highest performing 10 percent of our students, 30 to 50 percent lost ground as they moved from elementary to middle school or from middle to high school (Singal, 1991). Faculty at our most selective universities are dismayed by the "declining quality of student preparation" for those with the highest grade point averages (GPAs) (Hansen, 2013). In crucial areas like analytic reading and writing, the situation is pronounced (Dillon, 2004; Graff, 2003; Tucker; 2015).

Heaven help the rest. Tens of millions of less advantaged kids are deeply, even permanently, affected. Fewer than half of our students are reading at grade level by the end of 3rd grade, even in the higher achieving states (Wu, 2010). The other half won't learn near as much from their years in school, and they're four times as likely to drop out (Hernandez, 2012).

If we want to significantly improve educational outcomes and if we want to maximize efforts to make up for pandemic-era learning loss, it's imperative that all parties—educators, parents, the public, school boards—are sufficiently informed of these patterns. Only then can we work together to replace them with practices that would improve outcomes by an order of magnitude.

From Local Knowledge to National Improvement

Earlier, I shared that parents acquire a far more realistic view of their children's achievement when they receive accurate information about school and student performance.

These findings come from a study sponsored by several prestigious foundations with a vested interest in an educated workforce (Carnegie Corporation of New York, 2018). These foundations are convinced that we won't have better schools until we "give parents a complete and accurate picture of their children's achievement" and that this is the essential "first step to ensuring their academic success" (p. 1).

Commenting on this phenomenon, the Fordham Institute's Michael Petrilli (2017) laments how parents are "sorely misinformed" by the information they now receive from schools, like grossly inflated student grades and GPAs (p. 1). This discourages the demand for essential changes: "The message from most of [the school's] data points is 'your kid is doing fine!'" However, many aren't—and parents deserve to know this. Petrilli's hope, like mine, is that if enough families see that their children's likely future includes remedial education, then maybe they will start pushing their K–12 schools to do more to help prepare their kids for success.

Accurate knowledge of schooling is essential, but so is an acquaintance with powerful practices that have done so much to help schools such as those we'll learn about in the following chapters. We've been looking at parent perceptions as opposed to actual student attainment levels. What else should educators and the public know about current schooling—and its consequences?

What We Don't Know That Hurts Us

I invite you to carefully consider the implications of the following little-known facts about public education and their effect on our kids. I'll expand on each in coming chapters.

- As Richard Elmore told me over coffee at Harvard, "Effective practice is voluntary and therefore rare." Every credible study of schools demonstrates that the most crucial research-based methods are only implemented in a small minority of classrooms (Elmore, 1999–2000; Odden & Kelley, 2002; Willingham & Rotherham, 2020).

- Children in U.S. schools have about a 1 in 14 chance of being in an effective, intellectually stimulating classroom (Pianta et al., 2007).
- In the all-important early grades, students spend remarkably little time *either learning to read* or *actually reading*. About two-thirds of our lengthy literacy blocks make no contribution to student literacy (Ford & Opitz, 2002).
- There is a frightening correlation among illiteracy, dependence, and pathology: two-thirds of students who can't read by 5th grade end up on welfare or in jail. Sixty percent of prison inmates and 85 percent of youth in the criminal justice system are "functionally illiterate" (Kirkland, 2019).
- Every year, about 500 hours of class time are wasted, at every grade level and across all subjects, on activities that contribute virtually nothing to student knowledge or intellectual development (The New Teacher Project [TNTP], 2018).
- We have seen a dramatic collapse in academic standards in the last 25 years. Grades and graduation rates have soared even as actual rigor and achievement have declined (Tucker, 2015).
- Only one in three high school seniors reads proficiently, and even fewer are proficient in math. Achievement among struggling students was at a record low even before the COVID-19 pandemic (Sparks, 2020b).
- Seventy percent of students enter college upon high school graduation, but only 37 percent are college ready. The rate is much lower for poor students and students of color (Petrilli, 2016).
- High school graduates don't merely struggle. Most "hit an academic wall during their first year of college" in both reading and writing (Varlas, 2016, p. 1). This is even true for students entering the most prestigious institutions (Wahleithner, 2020).
- Only 13 percent of community college students graduate on time. More than 40 percent must take remedial courses, and fewer than 20 percent of those taking remedial courses graduate within five years (Vlasova, 2022).

- Despite massive infusions of funding in educational improvement, there has been no improvement in high school math or reading performance in more than 40 years. Millennials in the United States may be "the worst-educated workforce in the industrialized world" (Tucker, 2021, p. 1).
- Despite untold billions spent on literacy, the "bottom is falling out" for our lowest readers. In the last 10 years, these students have lost ground (Sparks, 2021, p. 1).
- Although general knowledge is the key to reading comprehension, students' knowledge of history, geography, and civics are at record lows (Wexler, 2020b).
- These realities have a crushing effect on underprivileged students. Of those who attend college, only 15 to 20 percent graduate within eight years (Petrilli, 2016).

Should educators and ordinary citizens care about the total impact of such facts? The answer is a resounding *yes*. So what must we do? As we saw in the field of medicine, K–12 must learn to "wash its hands"—to identify and implement the most incontrovertibly effective practices. It's that simple.

However, the buffer, which we'll revisit in Chapter 5, precludes this. It prevents a critical mass of the right people from grasping just how enormous and accessible this opportunity really is. I hope the schools described in the coming chapters will vividly illustrate this and inspire simple, powerful actions like those I'll recommend in the last chapter. In the next three chapters, we'll examine the most indispensable but rarely implemented elements of effective schooling, starting with curriculum.

2

Curriculum: The Foundation of Effective Education

What *we teach isn't some sidebar issue*
in American education; it is American education.

—David Steiner, executive director,
Johns Hopkins Institute for Education Policy

If even reasonably well taught, curriculum—"what we teach"—is the most fundamental, high-impact element of schooling. It's the foundation for all other elements.

If we want better schools, the most effective initial step we can take is to provide every teacher with a clear, easy-to-follow schedule of "what to teach and when"—an outline of the essential content, skills, and reading and writing assignments for each course, arranged in a sensible order in one- or two-week increments. This is not to say that I'm a fan of scripted, prepackaged, or agenda-driven curricula. Teachers need reasonable freedom to create and deliver the curriculum in their own language, and they need the opportunity to adjust, within limits, the pace of coverage (DuFour & Marzano, 2011; Schmoker, 2018).

In these fraught times, we shouldn't be paralyzed by the big arguments in English and social studies about what content to teach. It's enough for teachers to come to *provisional* agreements about certain *essential* core content that all agree to teach. This content should occupy between 60 and 80 percent of the overall course, which would afford teachers the time and opportunity to teach some of their preferred topics.

We can do this, as DuFour and others have demonstrated (Dufour et al., 2006; Schmoker, 2018). Consensus on the core can best be achieved by facilitators employing simple decision-making tools as teachers discuss and decide on major works of literature and on major epochs, events, and people to include in the history and civics curriculum. We can revisit and revise the curriculum every year or two.

There are fast, efficient ways for teachers to build such a curriculum for a given course in just a few hours. (See Schmoker, 2018, pp. 46–50, for a simple process for building sound curriculum in any course.) If we're smart, we will also develop common interim or unit assessments on the agreed-on content. For example, in English language arts, the primary assessments should focus on writing (a formal paper of a designated length) and speaking/discussion skills. Such interim assessments promote fidelity to the curriculum and enable teachers, in professional learning teams, to use collective assessment results as the basis for improvement efforts.

A coherent curriculum makes it vastly easier for teachers to build lessons that derive from it. We should remind teachers that their lessons need not be particularly elaborate or complex. Teachers can build them around versatile (but underappreciated) routine academic activities, such as close reading, note-taking, discussion, and writing about content—*in response to rich, open-ended questions or prompts.* (See Schmoker, 2018, pp. 94–95, as well as Chapters 4–7, for numerous examples.) Done right, these activities never become dull. Curriculum built around this core simplifies lesson planning and powerfully promotes students' intellectual and expressive capacities.

That's curriculum. And the case for its primacy is ironclad.

The Case for Curriculum

In a landmark issue of *American Educator* (2010–2011), multiple experts make the case for curriculum. Like no other factor, it lightens teachers' workloads, reduces their anxiety, and "brings coherence to the whole educational endeavor." A "mountain of real-world evidence" proves that "coherent, content-rich curriculum" is the single largest factor that promotes equity and higher achievement (p. 2). It also has a decisive effect on National Assessment of Educational Progress (NAEP) scores (Sahm, 2017).

For Doug Lemov, "Curriculum has been the most overlooked factor in the struggle for higher achievement. High-quality, knowledge-rich curriculum is key" (Hess, 2022, para. 15). Meta-analytic studies found it has a greater effect on learning than any other school factor (DuFour & Marzano, 2011). Coherent curriculum is the prime ingredient in effective schooling if, that is, it is generously imbued with opportunities to learn through purposeful reading, discussion, and writing (Conley, 2007).

The impact of a sound curriculum is 40 times as cost effective as class-size reduction (Wiener & Pimentel, 2017). It can make up for most of the learning deficits among entering kindergartners—deficits from which many students never recover (Darling-Hammond, 2010–2011). As David Steiner (2017) asserts,

> An education system without an effective instructional core is like a car without a working engine: It can't fulfill its function. No matter how much energy and money we spend working on systemic issues—school choice, funding, assessments, accountability, and the like—not one of these policies educates children. That is done only through curriculum and teachers: the material we teach and how effectively we teach it. (p. 1)

For the editors of *American Educator* (2010–2011), there can be "no educational equity" (p. 2) without coherent curriculum. What more do we need to convince us of curriculum's outsized importance?

In addition to these facts, there are compelling logical reasons why curriculum is central to achievement.

The Logic of Curriculum

There are several commonsense arguments for the power of clear, sequential teacher-generated curriculum:

1. It ensures common content and teacher expectations, as opposed to the "curricular chaos" that prevails in most schools—the startling variance in topics, rigor, and expectations among teachers of the same course in the same school (Marzano, 2003; Schmoker & Marzano, 1999). In the absence of such a curriculum, the content and quality of what children learn depend on which teacher they happen to get (DuFour & Marzano, 2011).

2. It ensures that students write and read in adequate amounts. With reasonable guidance, a decent curriculum is far more apt to include healthy amounts of writing, writing instruction, and high-quality, grade-level reading materials. In the absence of such specificity, writing is rare and text quality drifts downward; more than 80 percent of what students now read is written below their grade level (Mitchell, 2004; TNTP, 2018).

3. It greatly discourages the use of inferior materials (like worksheets) and inane activities that now occupy a large share of the school day (more on this in Chapters 2 and 3).

4. It enables administrators and evaluators to manage—in the best sense of that term—what gets taught in their school. It enables them to ensure that all students benefit from the teacher-generated skills and content deemed most important by faculty.

5. It saves teachers tremendous time in lesson planning and rescues them from falling back on popular but inferior programs, basal series, and activities gleaned from the internet.

6. It enables students to more easily acquire general knowledge, which is the key to reading comprehension (Hirsch, 2016;

Wexler, 2019). Social studies knowledge by itself—of history, geography, and civics—contributes decisively to gains in reading. This finding is among the most consequential educational research discoveries of recent decades (Terada & Merrill, 2020).

7. It's a nonnegotiable condition for productive teacher collaboration (DuFour & Marzano, 2011). Without a clear, sequential curriculum, teams of teachers cannot work productively to improve instructional delivery in team-based professional learning communities.

We must do more than merely *develop* curriculum. As Marzano (2003) makes clear, it must be *guaranteed*—that is, implemented consistently by all faculty. That requires administrative oversight and leadership.

Can most schools or districts presently guarantee the delivery of a reasonably high-quality curriculum? No. Again, however, absence equals opportunity. Because of curriculum's singular power, its introduction into any school tends to have a swift and "stunningly powerful" effect on achievement.

We've yet to fully grasp this fact—or act on it. The various buffers in our K–12 system have hidden this game-changing opportunity from view.

Behind the Buffer: Curricular Chaos

We live in an era of curricular chaos (Schmoker & Marzano, 1999). As I noted, each contributor to that special edition of *American Educator* lamented the maddening absence of curriculum in U.S. schools. Each author pleaded with educators to return curriculum to its supreme place in effective schooling.

That was 2011. Not much has changed (Hirsch, 2020). The blame for this "dirty little secret" isn't on teachers. It's on the education professionals who continue to regard curriculum as an afterthought (Pondiscio, 2016).

An example will suffice here to show what leaders can do if they put their minds to it. In the tours I conducted in that "high-achieving" district, a new superintendent made a bold move: She hired a reputable group to conduct an honest curriculum audit. What did it reveal? It showed that there was no curriculum operating in the school. Like the overwhelming majority of U.S. school districts, that district's so-called curriculum documents offered no clear guidance for what to teach and when to teach it. Therefore, most teachers ignored them. The report found no procedures for monitoring what was taught or for how teachers might teach that content; this was obvious from our tours. This contributed to another finding—that behind the district's respectable overall test scores, there was a large and growing sector of low-performing students and low-performing schools.

Happily, the superintendent shared the auditor's report with the school board. It broke through the buffer and disrupted the complacency in this highly reputed school system.

Every district in the United States should conduct such an honest audit, internally or externally. In most schools, it would reveal a tremendous need and an opportunity for improvement.

Let's now look at what my experience revealed to me—as a student teacher, teacher, consultant, and parent.

As a Student Teacher

During the first phase of my student teaching, my cooperating teacher suggested that I teach two sections on the novels of Charles Dickens to 10th graders. I assumed there would be a written guide, telling me which books to read and what kinds of papers students should write. There wasn't.

There was no curriculum, just a boilerplate paragraph describing each course, with no specifics whatsoever. My anxiety soared. My only hope was that I would learn how to teach these novels from my veteran mentor. I assumed that he would show students how to analyze literature, that he would lead meaningful discussions, and that he would teach the students how to write.

He did none of these things. He occasionally assigned readings, with no preparation or purpose given, followed by quizzes. The subsequent discussions were brief and aimless, with the same small handful of students doing the talking. On other days, he showed filmstrips or entire movies. In that nine-week period, he never taught writing and never had his high school students write more than a paragraph. So much for phase one of my student teaching experience.

In the next portion, I assisted two bright, big-hearted, junior high teachers as they team-taught a multiweek mythology unit. The professors at my college had described them in glowing terms. The teachers were committed, hard-working people. However, in the absence of any school or district curriculum—or any administrative guidance from school or district leadership—they had developed a bevy of "creative" activities, presumably to rescue English from the banalities of (mere) reading, discussion, and writing.

The majority of the unit had no relation to literacy. Students watched mythology-based Hollywood movies. They cut, sewed, and adorned old bedsheets to make Greek togas; they made head garlands out of paper leaves and wire hangers; and whole periods were spent mixing bowls of fruit salad (to mimic ambrosia, the food of the gods). At the end of the unit, students were given a single writing assignment, but with no instruction in what or how to write. I was tasked with grading their work without any guidance or criteria—except that no student should receive less than a *C*.

The next week was spent "publishing" these written assignments. We procured large rolls of colored paper and fabric from bolts in the art supply room, then helped each student unfurl and cut the paper into pages. The students then transcribed their stories onto the pages while chatting. They included title pages and dedications like "real" published books. Then they bound the pages with thread and placed them between cardboard covers they had previously adorned with colorful fabrics—and glitter.

Would parents, community members—or properly trained education professionals—not balk if they knew such activities constituted the bulk of an English class? There was no legitimate reading, writing, or discussion—only movies, fruit salad, and glitter.

This is what happens in the absence of curriculum. The integrity and substance of education gradually erode until they go off the rails. I saw the same chaos when I made the transition from student teacher to faculty member.

As a Teacher

I was ecstatic when I was offered my first teaching position at a brand-new high school, but I was taken aback when my department head asked me—a new, inexperienced teacher—to write the 9th grade English curriculum before school began that August. The school needed a curriculum to pass muster with the regional accrediting agency.

I teamed up with a colleague, and we beat one out with no guidance. It was a meaningless document, not a curriculum at all, just a list of grammatical skills and vague sentences about the importance of reading and writing. Still—please note—it passed muster with the accrediting agency with flying colors.

As far as I know, no one ever used our "curriculum," nor did anyone ever refer to it in a faculty or department meeting. We taught what and how we liked, with no supervision whatsoever. When I asked a veteran teacher at the school for guidance on how to teach my course, she simply told me to teach grammar skills from *Warriner's English Grammar and Composition* every day during first semester. For the second semester, she advised me to "use the lit book" (with excerpts and various activities). No one ever advised us to have students read entire books. I remember her response when I asked for guidance on writing; it was something like, "What? Teach writing? With our class loads?"

Years later at a different school, I asked this same question of another English department head. She said she rarely taught writing and wasn't about to ask her hardworking teachers to grade papers. Ironically, this was an *A+* school in an award-winning district that conducted periodic curriculum revisions. Again, these curricular documents were not legitimate curricula; they didn't even begin to help teachers know what to teach and when. Even a few chats in the teachers' lounge revealed that no one used these documents as a guide to what they taught. Teachers provided their own divergent sets of topics and activities—the "self-selected jumble" that has gone by the name of *curriculum* for more than half a century (Hirsch, 2020; Rosenholtz, 1991).

When I transitioned to the central office of this same district, I discovered that few teachers were even familiar with these curricula in any of the schools. Building administrators didn't monitor classrooms to ensure their use.

As a Consultant

A few years later, I did some consulting for a high school that had good scores and an excellent state rating despite its large proportion of low-performing students. It had a sterling reputation in the community. Our work began with a presentation in which I carefully defined curriculum and made the case for its supreme importance. In the course of the presentation, the faculty readily conceded that no such curriculum existed in their district and that they were left to wing it. They agreed it was time to build a curriculum for each course, using simple templates that would make the work go quickly.

The need to do this was vividly apparent on our classroom tours. We often found students engaged in activities such as coloring in maps of the states in a U.S. history class—in groups, while chatting. In another class, the teacher read the newspaper every day while students completed worksheets. This had gone on for years.

In an advanced science class, students chatted as they labeled the parts of a microscope on a worksheet. A 10-minute task at best, it occupied an entire period. Subsequent observations confirmed the same pattern of low-value activities and worksheets, which couldn't possibly have had a place in any legitimate curriculum. When we met with the teacher, she told us that you cannot create a curriculum for science because science knowledge changes so quickly. We tried to hide our amazement and asked if there weren't certain enduring concepts—such as cell structure or anatomy—that she should necessarily include in her biology course. She wouldn't concede this. This teacher wasn't only a teacher—she was the head of the science department.

A few days later, the superintendent called the principal. His message was this: "You've upset some people with this talk about curriculum. You need to keep your people happy." Again, all of this was happening in an *A+* school where the preceding principal had received awards for school leadership. The buffer hides such ironies, which are in line with Elmore's research on administrative priorities.

As a Parent

Around this time, my daughters entered a new high school. On parent night, one of my daughters' English teachers distributed a syllabus. It was encouraging: it contained assurances that students would be preparing for college writing through "weekly writing assignments." My wife and I were delighted.

Alas, it was not to be. By Thanksgiving, my daughter had not been asked to complete anything longer than a paragraph or two. This led to a meeting with the teacher and principal just before the end of first semester. The principal had no idea if or how much writing students were assigned in English courses. When I referred to the "weekly writing assignments" in the syllabus, the teacher admitted she hadn't gotten around to teaching writing yet (it was almost midyear). The meeting went nowhere. The content of the next semester was even more concerning; instead of reading and writing, students spent serious time producing a "literary scrapbook," the dubious qualities of which I'll describe in the chapter on literacy.

Such activities could never populate any legitimate curriculum developed by a team of professionals with adequate guidance about the need to include sufficient amounts of reading, discussion, and writing. This was, after all, an English class. Most importantly, the bulk of what the teacher actually taught was nowhere in the syllabus she distributed on parent night. Her syllabus and parent presentation were a ruse—and a highly effective buffer between us parents and the substance of her course.

The instructor, by the way, was a recent Teacher of the Year award recipient.

In another daughter's class, her history teacher would simply lecture and frequently digress from the subject matter—for weeks, sometimes months, without giving any tests or quizzes. Students never knew what they would be tested on; even conscientious students would perform well on some tests and inexplicably fail others. That teacher was the history department chair.

I could go on. Suffice it to say that these are not atypical examples. Yes, there are fine teachers in our schools, and my daughters had several, but the best ones—when I've gotten to know them—agree that the activities I've described are exceedingly common in schools because there's no credible, teacher-friendly curriculum in place that would act as a guardrail against such excesses.

Who Knows What to Teach?

Over the years, I've been invited to review curricula with the administrative cabinets of numerous districts, including the largest in the United States. In perusing them, it becomes apparent that the documents don't answer the simple question "What essential knowledge and skills should teachers teach in the next week or two?" After a little probing, district administrators concede (and their teachers admit to me) the staggering variation in what kids are taught in the same subject at the same grade level.

I'm reminded of a teacher's poignant, anonymously written account that appeared in *American Educator* (2010–2011). The teacher writes about the shock of arriving to her first school and realizing she had no curriculum to work from. At the end of her new teacher orientation, it hit her: The administration and her department chair were more concerned with her knowing the location of the faculty restroom than with what she would be teaching her students that year (Second-Year Teacher, 2008).

Does formal research confirm these unsettling accounts?

Curricular Chaos: The Research

Every study, spanning decades, confirms that the *actual, taught* curriculum rarely derives from any organized schedule of content and skills. It's actually quite the opposite. What gets taught is usually a "self-selected jumble" (Rosenholtz, 1991). It's typically a set of topics and activities reflecting the preferences of each individual teacher, who "can teach pretty much whatever they want, using pretty much whatever materials they want" (Finn, 2017, p. 1).

Most educators know this, and it frustrates them. A popular curriculum expert used to regularly ask audiences of teachers and administrators what a *curriculum document* was. After a beat, she would say "a well-intended fiction." A burst of knowing laughter would follow.

We live in an era of curricular chaos (Schmoker & Marzano, 1999) and curricular anarchy (Marshall, 2003). This distinguishes the United States from education systems in the most improved, highest-achieving nations (*American Educator*, 2010–2011; Ripley, 2013; Stoltzfus, 2017).

Few people know this. I've spoken to a multitude of parents who assume their children's teachers work from an organized, sequential program of study. As our best researchers remind us, this is a "gravely misleading myth" (Dufour & Marzano, 2011, p. 90). It's not uncommon to find teachers of the same course, in the same school, teaching entirely different topics. This leaves huge holes in what students are taught (Marzano, 2003). Education professor David Berliner and colleagues (Berliner, 1984) found alarming differences among teachers in the same school; for example, an elementary teacher devoted 27 times as much time to science as a teacher down the hall. None of the administrators were aware of this.

We've spent decades developing state standards documents. These have not resulted in the creation of, much less the delivery of, decent curricula in U.S. schools. In sum, with regard to what is arguably the most foundational, high-leverage element of good schooling, we aren't even out of the blocks. Most schools have gone curriculum-free for decades. The cost of this failure—and the opportunity it bespeaks—is inestimable.

Here's what's remarkable. If you survey the contents of educational publications, you will seldom come across an article or a pattern of articles that reflects an awareness of this crisis—or the monumental opportunity it represents. There's little demand, in the name of student learning and quality of life, to make curriculum our number-one priority right now. Our kids pay a dear price for our complacence.

Again, is the public or the education establishment even aware of this opportunity? Has anyone anywhere strongly made the case for curriculum, enabling us to take the full measure of its value and the chance it gives us to make swift, significant improvements to school quality?

When Coherence Replaces Chaos

Perhaps the most powerful case for curriculum is looking at the schools that have committed to it.

Europe

For decades, French students learned from a content-rich national curriculum. As a result, students at every demographic level enjoyed high rates of success. In the 1980s, though, the country abandoned that curriculum. The result was "an astonishingly steep decline" in overall achievement, but especially among the poorest of France's students, as "inequality increased dramatically" (Hirsch, 2016, pp. 3–4).

Germany and Sweden made the same error, but unlike France, they corrected course. In the early 2000s, both countries abandoned their national "shared knowledge" course curricula for ones that catered to individual student interests and abilities. In the wake of this,

German student achievement declined from well above average to well below average on the venerable Programme for International Student Assessment (PISA), a more robust assessment of knowledge, analysis, and reasoning than U.S. state assessments. As a result, Germany reinstituted its former curriculum. Within a few years, they improved from 22nd to 10th place on the 2018 PISA. The United States ranks 24th on that assessment (Hirsch, 2020).

During the same period, Sweden also saw its PISA ranking tumble—from 9th to 27th place—when they abandoned their common curriculum. Once restored, Swedish achievement rebounded strongly; in three years, it rose from 27th to 17th place (Hirsch, 2020).

United States

Here in the United States, a network of private schools replaced their "hodge-podge" of offerings with coherent grade-by-grade curriculum. In just two years, they were able to double the number of students achieving proficiency in English and triple the number who succeeded in math (Sahm, 2017).

Some entire states made steady, sizeable gains when they instituted standards and assessments that facilitated the development and implementation of curricula. Massachusetts students are among the highest achieving in the United States. It wasn't always so. Measurable improvements occurred in the early 1990s when reformers were inspired by the curriculum-focused work of E. D. Hirsch (Stern, 2009). The state's revised standards were clear and challenging and, most important, had a healthy writing component. All this supported the sole purpose of standards documents: to make it easier for districts to develop a clear, teacher-friendly curriculum.

By 1993, Massachusetts's SAT scores began to rise. They did so for 13 consecutive years. Scores on the challenging NAEP shot up as well. By 2005, Massachusetts students were near the top and became the first to score best in the nation in all four major NAEP categories: reading, writing, mathematics, and science. They repeated the feat in 2007,

2009, and 2011. Their ranking on international assessments also rose commensurately (Glenn, 2018).

Mather Elementary is the oldest elementary school in the Boston Public Schools system. For nine years, it was mired in low achievement—until the principal charged the faculty to build and implement a home-grown, coherent curriculum based on Massachusetts standards, with its strong emphasis on writing in all subject areas. As a result, the school made the largest gains in the district. Mather rose from the bottom to the top third in achievement on the Massachusetts Comprehensive Assessment System in one school year (Marshall, 2003).

Brockton High School is the largest high school in the state. It was once among the very lowest-achieving schools. The then–social studies chair (and future principal), Sue Szachowicz, gathered a small team to discuss how to make improvements. They made a momentous decision to eschew educational fads altogether—particularly differentiated, personalized learning (more on this in Chapter 5). Instead, the leadership team helped teachers develop a clear, emphatically literacy-rich curriculum in every subject. As Szachowicz mentioned to me in her office, they did what Elmore tells us is so very rare in our schools: The leadership team "manage[d] the instructional core" (Elmore, 1999–2000). They "monitored like crazy" to ensure the curriculum was actually being implemented in every classroom. If it wasn't, crucial conversations occurred.

There is no substitute for such leadership.

Results came hard and fast. At the end of the first year's effort, the commissioner of education for Massachusetts informed the leadership team that they had made the largest gains in the state. It didn't stop there. In just six years, Brockton's achievement rose from near bottom in state standings to the top 10 percent (Ferguson, 2016; Szachowicz, personal communication). I'll share more about Brockton in coming chapters.

Now consider a diverse high school in my own Arizona community with over a 90 percent poverty rate. It was in danger of closing because of its perennially low math scores. The math department made the fortuitous decision to develop, for the first time, clear, agreed-on curriculum maps for each math course. They developed these by themselves in just a few hours. Consequently, scores rose significantly in one year. They also rose in the second year, at the end of which I attended an awards ceremony that recognized the faculty for being among three schools that made the largest math gains in the state.

In Mead Valley Elementary School in Riverside County, California, 95 percent of students receive free or reduced-price lunch. Despite these challenges, the school made powerful gains when it implemented a common curriculum and common assessments for every course and grade level with the assistance of author and consultant Doug Reeves. Significantly, Mead Valley's curriculum was literacy-rich and imbued with daily writing activities and opportunities for students to read common grade-level texts.

The school's improvements were swift and steady. In four years, its Academic Performance Index (API) score for reading and math soared from 450 to 695. After three more years, it rose to 774, a score on par with much wealthier suburban schools in the area (Reeves, 2007).

A Mighty Pair

In the next chapter, we'll look at a variety of schools in which the impact of a common curriculum was particularly pronounced because it was (as any bona fide curriculum must be) literacy rich. Curriculum and literacy are richly entwined; neither is legitimate without the other. High-quality curriculum, by definition, must contain generous, specified amounts of literary and content-rich texts across subject areas. Together, they build the knowledge base so crucial to reading comprehension—and to academic and life success.

What unfortunate facts about literacy instruction now hide from us behind the buffer? What would happen if we restored the most crucial, traditional aspects of literacy to their proper place in the curriculum?

How to Manage Curriculum: Action Questions for Leaders

- Have you conducted an honest audit to assess whether a clear, coherent, literacy-rich curriculum is in place for every course in your school(s)?
- If not, do you have a plan to ensure such a curriculum is in place by the beginning of the coming semester? (For detailed instructions on how to rough these out in as little as a couple of hours per course, see Schmoker, 2018.)
- Have you presented a thorough case for the power of coherent curriculum to your faculty—and reinforced its importance regularly?
- Have you developed a system for administrators and instructional coaches to monitor curriculum to ensure that teachers are actually implementing it?

3

Literacy: The Engine of Equity

Students develop deep conceptual knowledge in a discipline only by using the habits of reading, writing, talking, and thinking, which that discipline values and uses.

—Stephanie McConachie and colleagues

Literacy is the soul of education and is integral to curriculum. To impart it to all students, we need to be clear about what it is and expose the numerous obstacles to literacy in our schools.

First, let's not overcomplicate it. As Thomas Friedman (2005) writes, the world of the future will be run by those who excel at "plain old reading and writing" (p. 353), or, as Doug Lemov put it in a recent interview, students should "read and read and read, write and write and write" (Hess, 2022).

If we care about our kids—and about equity—we owe every student abundant daily opportunities to read, discuss, and write about generous amounts of fiction and nonfiction across the disciplines. As Robert Pondiscio (2021a) notes, "Any discussion about 'equity' in education that is not first and foremost a discussion about literacy is unserious" (p. 1). Giving *every* student such opportunities to read, write, and discuss is the near opposite of what occurs in schools today.

Let's start by examining the fundamental elements of literacy and how to teach them. To become literate, students must

- **Learn systematic phonics.** Teaching phonics benefits all students—provided we don't elongate or devote excessive time to it. If teachers teach phonics intensively and properly in kindergarten and 1st grade, few students will need heavy doses beyond 1st grade. Phonics, of course, is not a literacy program (Willingham, 2018).

- **Read generous amounts of text.** This includes books, stories, articles, and poems in students' English classes, as well as various articles and textbook selections in their social studies, science, and elective courses. Texts should be at grade level to expose students to increasingly complex content and vocabulary. Some texts should be read slowly and analytically; teachers must show students explicitly how to do such reading, which varies by discipline (see Shanahan & Shanahan, 2017, for guidance on such instruction; Schmoker, 2018, Chapters 4–7).

- **Write frequently,** in both short and long formats and in formal and less formal modes. Students should write daily and liberally about what they're reading and learning (Graham, 2019). They should be taught to write increasingly longer, more sophisticated papers at each grade level, culminating in clear, well-organized, multipage documents by the time they enter middle school. Importantly: Good writing instruction *does not require teachers to spend unreasonable amounts of time grading papers*; improvements in writing come mostly from effective instruction and not from meticulously correcting student errors (see "Write More, Grade Less" at http://mikeschmoker.com/write-more.html). Explicit writing instruction is effective at any age and with all student populations (Harris et al., 2008).

- **Participate frequently in purposeful discussions** driven by relevant, provocative open-ended questions in English language arts, social studies, science, and beyond. If we want students to acquire vital speaking, listening, presenting, and interactive skills, teachers must provide them with explicit instruction and coaching in how to speak clearly, audibly, and concisely about what they're reading. I can't overstate the academic, personal, and workplace benefits of these skills.

This is literacy: lots of reading, discussion, and writing built around higher-order questions that lend purpose to studies every hour, every day. Literacy is arguably the engine of curriculum and learning in most disciplines. Each of the four elements I've listed makes us smarter; in combination, they make us *way* smarter—and better workers and citizens.

The Multiple Cases for Literacy

Once students have mastered the phonetic code, they should begin reading, discussing, and writing about what they read. These may be the most valuable educational activities we know and the key to cultivating thoughtfulness. To be truly literate is to be educated. As E. D. Hirsch (2010) writes, "Literacy is the most important single goal of schooling in any nation. . . . The earnings gap between racial and ethnic groups in the U.S. largely disappears when language competence in standard English is factored in" (p. 31).

On the other hand, the failure to acquire literacy skills is devastating. As the former heads of the National Associations of Elementary and Secondary School Principals (Ferrandino & Tirozzi, 2004) point out, "Underdeveloped literacy skills are the number one reason why students are retained, assigned to special education, given long-term remedial services, and why they fail to graduate high school" (p. 1).

The Case for Reading

Reading probably has more effect on a student's intellectual growth, knowledge base, and test scores than any other activity. It nurtures the ability to speak, write, think, and empathize. Historian and philosopher of education Jacque Barzun (1991) is emphatic: "No subject of study is as important as reading. . . . All other intellectual powers depend on it" (p. 21). As Michael Petrilli (2021) also notes, "Reading ability has been shown to be twice as predictive of positive long-term outcomes as math scores" (para. 9).

We still underestimate the power of large amounts of "plain old reading" (Friedman, 2005). Just three to four weeks of effective, full-day reading and reading instruction would enable an average student to achieve an entire year of academic growth (Haycock, 2005). Evidence shows that significant increases in time spent reading would reduce, if not eliminate, our most stubborn achievement gaps (Anderson, Wilson, & Fielding, 1988; Sparks, Patton, & Murdoch, 2013).

In his bestselling book *When Breath Becomes Air*, the late Paul Kalanithi (2016) describes how liberal amounts of reading compensated for the inferior education he received in the rural town in which he grew up. It enabled him to attend Stanford University, then Yale University Medical School, after which he became an accomplished neurosurgeon.

As we'll see later in this chapter, increases in student reading have led to significant academic and intellectual growth for countless individuals, classrooms, and schools.

Moreover, numerous researchers have found that reading cultivates social and emotional capacities (Schmidt, 2020). These include patience, empathy, and understanding diverse peoples, cultures, and viewpoints. Literature and history enable us to appreciate such multiple perspectives, and they create opportunities for exercising empathic skills that promote understanding and tolerance. George R. R. Martin (2011) sums it up, saying, "A reader lives a thousand lives before he dies. The man who never reads lives only one" (p. 2).

But reading isn't enough. As Francis Bacon wrote in 1597, "Reading maketh a full man; conference a ready man; and writing an exact man." How important is "conference"—that is, school-based discussion? The topic deserves far more attention than it has received.

The Case for Discussion—And Its Role in a Democracy

Discussion profoundly develops and refines our intellectual and expressive capacities. It has never been so important for us to make ample room for informed, logical, civil discourse in the school day. "Free human dialog," according to Neil Postman (1996), "lies at the heart of education" (p. 165). Through discussion, students learn to process and compare their thoughts with others as they become increasingly effective listeners, speakers, and citizens.

Gerald Graff (2003), the former president of the Modern Language Association, is an advocate for the cardinal importance of argument literacy. He writes that "Talk—about books and subjects—is as important educationally as are the books and subjects themselves" (p. 9).

David Conley's (2005) team at the University of Oregon set out to discover precisely what experiences students need to have K–12 to thrive in college. Among the most important were abundant opportunities to share their interpretations and opinions in "classroom discussion and debates" in which they learn "to support their arguments and provide evidence of their assertions" (p. 81).

Mike Rose (1989) writes in a similar vein that education itself is "an initiation into a variety of powerful ongoing discussions . . . where students learn to talk about what they're learning: to test their ideas, reveal their assumptions, talk through the places where new knowledge clashes with ingrained belief" (pp. 192–193). These skills have wide academic and career applications. Mary Ehrenworth (2017) of Columbia Teachers College writes that civil "argumentation is not just a skill for language arts classrooms—it is also a pathway to success in virtually every academic discipline" (p. 35).

John Almarode (in Ferlazzo, 2021), professor of science education at James Madison University, points to the importance of discussion in science, technology, engineering, and math (STEM). He's worth quoting at length:

> Getting my learners to talk through concepts, practices, and understandings had the greatest impact on their science learning. Not

laboratories, demonstrations, worksheets, or movies. In high school physics, critical conversations allowed my learners to deeply think about the physical principles involved in a problem, the different approaches to solving that problem, and then making meaning of the solution within the context of scientific phenomena. This is not simply a hunch. Year after year, my learners and I documented the greatest gains in their learning as a result of student talk. (para. 1)

For all this, the greatest value of civil, logical discussion may be civic and humanistic. In words more urgent than ever, Mary Ehrenworth (2017) writes, "There has never been a more important time to teach young people to suspend judgment, weigh evidence, consider multiple perspectives, and speak up with wisdom and grace on behalf of themselves" (p. 1).

If we value democracy and civic comity, we must provide students with frequent opportunities to develop these social and emotional skills and dispositions through civil dialogue and discussion, including all-important listening skills. We've all seen how students often acquire fixed opinions during their school years and how this can drift into extremism and intolerance as they enter adult life. Free discussion enables students to refine— and moderate—their thinking as they listen and reflect on perspectives they haven't considered. This is how we acquire wisdom and maturity.

Two Northwestern University professors, Gary Saul Morson and Morton Schapiro (2021), have developed a course to promote such open, respectful discussion. It's been a huge success. For them, "Genuine dialogue is the lifeblood of democracy, requiring an unending exchange—and testing—of ideas and ideological fashions" (para. 13). It's paramount that we provide such experiences in K–12 classrooms— not to indoctrinate but to impart the discipline of thoughtful dialogue. If comity, community, and good government matter, then school must be a place where students feel safe expressing and listening to divergent views—right, left, and center—in a spirit of honest inquiry.

Morson and Schapiro's conclusions echo the work of social commentator and onetime U.S. presidential adviser Christopher Lasch

(1995), who believes that free, disciplined argument is at the heart of an education for democracy:

> It is only by subjecting our preferences and projects to the test of debate that we come to understand what we know and what we still need to learn. Until we have to defend our opinions in public, they remain opinions . . . half-formed convictions based on random impressions and unexamined assumptions. (p. 71)

K–12 education is exquisitely positioned to promote democracy, tolerance, and wisdom through free, civil dialogue long before students graduate from high school. College is too late—*way* too late—to cultivate these capacities. Finally, but significantly, corporate recruiters report that the ability to speak, listen, and write is the most sought-after skill set (Hurley, 2015); communication skills ranked *twice as high* as other job-related skills.

The Case for Writing

Writing is richly enhanced through discussion—and it enhances discussion skills in return.

It's an especially potent, overlooked element of an education. We've done a regrettable job of ensuring that teachers acquire a deep understanding of its power to equip students for life, work, and citizenship. This has become acutely apparent at a time when some educators appear to believe that writing programs such as ChatGPT can somehow obviate the need for frequent daily writing—and writing instruction. This is a gross misconception.

For instructional expert Doug Lemov (cited in Hochman & Wexler, 2017), writing is unique among the core aspects of a high-quality education. As he puts it,

> If I could wave a magic wand over America's schools and cause one change that would drive the most demonstrable improvement to learning and achievement, I would almost certainly wave that wand and conjure up small bursts of intense, reflective, high-quality writing in every class period or every hour across America's schools. (p. xvii)

David Conley (2007), an expert on what college demands of students, hits almost the same note: "If we could institute only one change to make students more college ready, it should be to increase the amount and quality of writing students are expected to produce" (p. 4). Likewise, here's what the late researcher Robert Slavin had to say:

> The ability to express ideas in writing is one of the most important of all skills. Good writing is a mark of an educated person, and perhaps for that reason it is one of the most important skills sought by employers and higher education institutions. (Slavin et al., 2019, p. 5)

Gerald Graff (2003) points out that writing "comes into play in every field" (p. 22), and writing expert Steve Graham (2019) notes that

> Writing is a fundamental skill. Writers use this versatile skill to learn new ideas, persuade others, record information, create imaginary worlds, express feelings, entertain others, heal psychological wounds, chronicle experiences, and explore the meaning of events and situations. (p. 1)

Graham adds that the inability to write, which plagues so many of our high school graduates, "exacts a toll . . . on academic, occupational, and personal attainments" (p. 1). That's the fate, Graham informs us, of two-thirds of U.S. students.

The Case for Writing—And Thinking

The connection between effective writing and thinking grows out of the work of a legion of researchers, going back decades. More than any other activity, writing helps us develop and refine thought. As Graham (2019) writes, "Writing allows us to connect, analyze, organize, and express ideas" (p. 1). Through writing, students "make knowledge their own" and "rework raw information and dimly understood concepts" into language others can understand (National Commission on Writing, 2003, p. 9). For Ted Sizer, a giant in the early school reform movement, writing is the very "litmus paper of thought" and should therefore occupy "the very center of schooling" (cited in Marino, 1988, p. 20). According to former Nebraska senator Bob Kerrey, more than

90 percent of midcareer professionals say that writing is crucial to their daily work. It cultivates the "most valuable job attribute of all: a mind equipped to think" (National Commission on Writing, 2003, p. 11).

In "The Learning Power of Writing" (Walshe, 1987), one expert writes that we "shouldn't hesitate to describe writing as incredible or miraculous . . . a technology which enables thought to operate much more deeply than it normally does during conversation or inward reflection" (p. 22). Writing enables students to "contemplate thought . . . until it becomes the best thinking of which they are capable" (Ede, 1987, p. 22). Other scholars find that writing "facilitates reflection upon the ramifications of an idea and allows for evaluation of a standpoint" by forcing us to carefully examine, then reevaluate, the first, often *un*examined thoughts that enter our heads (Kuhrt & Farris, 1990, p. 437). As Jacques Barzun (1991) points out, the process of writing is the best-known means of curbing the mind's natural disinclination to logic, order, and precision. Finally, writing expert William Zinsser (1988) notes that writing is primarily an exercise in logic. Such exercise is paramount if we want our students to become rational, respectful, objective citizens because, Zinsser continues,

> Meaning is remarkably elusive. . . . Writing enables us to find out what we know—and what we don't know—about whatever we're trying to learn. Putting an idea into written words is like defrosting the windshield: The idea, so vague out there in the murk, slowly begins to gather itself into a sensible shape . . . all of us know this moment of finding what we really want to say by trying in writing to say it. (pp. 14–16)

That moment of intellectual discovery, clarity, and precise expression is at the heart of an education.

Writing also promotes social and emotional self-discovery. It enables us to sort through and clarify our thoughts and emotions and thus enables us to achieve control over them. In her book *Write for Your Life*, Anna Quindlen (2022) suggests that "writing, for anyone, for everyone . . . can normalize the abnormal and feed the spirit." It can be a powerful means of "understanding yourself, hearing your own voice,

[and] puzzling out" who you are and what you want to become. It also affords us "a safe vantage point" from which to regard our struggles, insecurities, and disappointments (pp. 9–10).

These are the immense, manifold benefits of writing. No AI program (e.g., ChatGPT) will ever replace writing's most critical functions—to magnify our ability to generate, formulate, and refine thought in our own way and in our own voice.

For all this, here's a brutal fact: The case for writing gets hardly a mention in teacher and administrative preparation. Neither our prospective nor our practicing teachers are implored to include ample amounts of "reflective, high-quality writing in every class period or every hour across America's schools" (Lemov, cited in Hochman & Wexler, 2017, p. xvii).

Our failure to make the case for writing has left it exposed to specious ideological attacks. The written word is now being assailed by some scholars as overemphasized, even "damaging." They would have us reduce the already miniscule amounts of time and emphasis it gets in school (McWhorter, 2021). These thinkers, according to *The New York Times* (Bergner, 2021), dismiss the importance of writing and, with it, the intellectual capacities it powerfully cultivates: rational thought and an objective, scientific disposition. These are, of course, critical elements of a high-quality education and crucial to career success. We need to resist this anti-intellectual trend with logic and evidence. We must make the case for writing early and often for all educators.

Curriculum and literacy are mutually reinforcing. Our goal should be to create a literacy-rich curriculum in which students learn ample amounts of content through abundant amounts of reading, discussion, and writing. To achieve this, we'd be wise to embrace Richard Allington's (2011) sensible guideline: Students should read for at least 60 minutes each day and write for at least 40 minutes during the school day across disciplines. Writing expert Steve Graham (2019) recommends 60 minutes of writing daily.

We need to interlace reading and writing with liberal amounts of discussion, which helps students process what they read and is excellent preparation for writing. Doing so would propel learning, student engagement, and student success to new heights, as we'll see in a moment. Moreover, there's more than enough time in the school day to ensure such allotments.

Behind the Buffer: The Illusion of Literacy

Do we currently devote adequate time or emphasis to these crucial elements of literacy? Not even close.

Anyone who visits classrooms knows that students spend only token amounts of the school day reading, writing, and meaningfully discussing what they read. This explains why so many millions of students struggle and why a sizeable portion reach high school barely literate. It explains why about one in five students in the United States is functionally illiterate—that is, reading below a 5th grade level (*Huff-Post*, 2014).

Remember the upside here: The most substantial improvements occur where performance levels are low and superior practices replace the most common but inferior practices. By these criteria and in every area of literacy, the opportunity for improvement is vast.

Elementary Literacy: It's About Time

The ability to read adequately by the end of 3rd grade is crucial. Those who cannot will eventually struggle with reading through high school and are four times as likely to drop out (Sparks, 2020a). There is a direct correlation—a pipeline—between illiteracy and antisocial behavior (Hernandez, 2012).

Only about half of our students read at grade level, according to their own state tests; on the more authentic National Assessment of Educational Progress (NAEP), only one in three students reads at grade level (National Center for Education Statistics, 2020). These failure rates are wholly unnecessary. The proportion of literate high school graduates would soar if we implemented proven practices,

starting in the early grades. If we coupled those practices with generous amounts of reading and writing, almost every child could be reading at grade level by the end of 1st grade—and virtually all of them by
2nd or 3rd grade (Allington, 2011; Barshay, 2020).

The International Literacy Association (in Sawchuck & Schwartz,
2019) now firmly endorses systematic and explicit phonics for all students. The key is to ensure that an overemphasis on phonics doesn't
crowd out other crucial elements of literacy or instruction in science
and social studies content, which are essential to comprehension. If
properly taught (with any decent phonics program), students only
need about 25 minutes of intensive phonics instruction each day for
about 100 days (Barshay, 2020; Englemann, Haddox, & Bruner, 1983).
That leaves large amounts of time every day for students to read, discuss, and write about fiction and nonfiction. Alarmingly, and despite
this emergent consensus, a mere 22 percent of kindergarten, 1st grade,
and 2nd grade teachers believe that phonics should be taught explicitly. Many—68 percent—still subscribe to some version of the widely
discredited three-cueing system, in which students are taught to read
by looking at pictures or guessing at word meanings based on context
(Barshay, 2020; *EdWeek* Research Center, 2020).

We won't see large improvements in early-grade reading until this
changes—and only if we pair phonics with big increases in the other
elements of literacy. This may sound obvious until you look at what
goes on in most early-grade classrooms. Even solid phonics instruction
is seldom accompanied by liberal, daily opportunities for students to
read, talk, and write in response to open-ended questions about fiction
and nonfiction. Even as students are learning phonics, they should,
as soon as possible, be reading along with the teacher for extended
periods. This expands their vocabulary and knowledge base, fortifies
comprehension, and consolidates phonetic knowledge.

The average reading block already affords ample time for this.
Unfortunately, teachers typically expend this valuable time on misguided practices and routines. Let's look at one such practice that
reveals the magnitude of the problem—and offers a prodigious opportunity for improvement.

The "Crayola Curriculum" in Elementary Schools

Years ago, I was invited to tour a high-poverty school with a number of education professors. The school had just won a prestigious award for its exemplary staff development program. As we toured the school during the reading block, I expected to see exemplary instruction. Instead, I noticed that in most classrooms, students were coloring. Some were drawing and then coloring in what they had drawn for extended periods of time. (I circled back to several classrooms to confirm this.)

Afterward, we gathered in one of the classrooms to share perceptions. With increasing unease, I listened as my colleagues delivered glowing encomiums concerning what we had just observed. I gingerly inquired if the professional development had led to any measurable increase in reading levels. After an awkward moment, one of the administrators replied that no, there hadn't been any measurable increase, not with the hardships kids faced in this high-poverty school. I then asked if anyone happened to notice that in almost every classroom, students were . . . coloring. This was met with some mumbled concessions. No one denied this was the case.

As a result of this experience, I started touring early-grade classrooms in schools around the United States. The pattern was unmistakable, and the coloring ubiquitous.

Others were noting this as well. The research teams of Kati Haycock (2005), then president of the Washington-based Education Trust, found that students spent more time coloring than on any other activity during the literacy block. Another study revealed that in a two-and-a-half-hour block, students often spent only 10 minutes reading (Calkins, Montgomery, & Santman, 1998). Ford and Opitz (2002) confirmed these findings, noting that about two-thirds of a typical early-grade reading period was spent on "cut, color, paste" activities.

These findings are shocking, but in keeping with our theme, they are brimming with opportunity. Ponder this: By design, schools now devote the first two to three hours of the morning, when children are fresh and learning is optimal, to literacy. Yet students spend a majority of that time on activities that contribute little or nothing to genuine literacy. If we repurposed that time, we could *double or triple* the time allotted to reading, writing, and discussion and to social studies and science content, which contribute so much to comprehension (Wexler, 2019). That's enough to dramatically narrow every kind of literacy and opportunity gap.

The prevalence of coloring is the kind of little-known fact that makes me so sanguine about the potential for sweeping improvements to educational quality. It's why I decided to write an article titled "The Crayola Curriculum" (Schmoker, 2001) for *Education Week*. I anticipated a backlash. It never came. The response to the article was enormous and almost universally positive. In an email, Harry Wong said he had noted this trend for years and joked that he would soon invest in Crayola stock. Carol Jago, then president of the National Council of Teachers of English (NCTE), confirmed that this was a national phenomenon and later used the term in an interview with *USA Today* for an article they titled "The Crayola Curriculum Takes Over" (Harrington-Lueker, 2002).

It's not just coloring. As Ford and Opitz discovered, the early-grade reading curriculum is packed with arts and crafts projects, which might be wonderful for art class but have no relation to reading or other academic content. This well-concealed bank of ill-used time is among the richest overlooked opportunities for improvement in all of education.

Arts and Crafts—Or Literacy and Learning?

In his article "Lost in Action," Gilbert Sewall (2000) describes activities he encountered while touring U.S. classrooms. He writes of how students spent some 20 hours on shoebox projects and maybe one hour on academic work; of students making photo montages and posters of the Eiffel Tower and Notre Dame Cathedral—instead of learning how to speak, read, and write French. These "time-consuming and trivializing activities," he writes, "are displacing the cultivation of active minds" (p. 1).

Many observers have agreed that there is no reading in the reading curriculum. Instead, students make game boards, 3D cardboard dioramas, posters, and decorative mobiles (Calkins, Montgomery, & Santman, 1998). Reading expert Elaine McEwan (in Vail, 2001) describes students in a low-performing school spending a total of 37 hours on the construction of a papier-mâché dinosaur. "Those kids," she writes, "couldn't read, but they spent all that time messing with chicken wire and wheat paste" (p. 2).

Education writer Jennifer Gonzalez (2016) describes the projects and activities her own children completed, as well as a multiweek history unit she observed in which students used the majority of their time to make and paint (once again) papier-mâché objects. The students then spent days preparing and presenting slideshow presentations that lacked any substantial learning. Such stuff, she found, impresses evaluators and administrators who only see that the students are "engaged" (that unfortunate, elastic word) and that such diversions are "really fun and the kids loved it" (pp. 3–4).

More recently, Gonzalez invited instructional expert Angela Peery (2021) to write an entry for her blog. Peery shared her observations of teaching in several states both before and during the COVID-19 pandemic. She is distressed by the same unproven instructional fads, the overreliance on worksheets, "the arts and crafts activities, and the paucity of authentic reading and writing activities." Notes Peery,

> Time and time again, teachers have turned to methods and tasks that don't work well but are easy to orchestrate. There is *less writing* . . . There is *more cutting, coloring, and pasting,* mostly at the elementary level. Teachers are showing a lot of YouTube videos without discussing them. There are *more worksheet packets than I've ever seen.* And, tragically, there is *too much passive screen time.* (para. 5; emphasis mine)

There's a long history of such activities, which persist because they remain hidden—or unacknowledged. I'm reminded of Harper Lee's (1960) striking passage in *To Kill a Mockingbird* about young Scout's school experience, probably reflective of Lee's own. Scout regrets her education in which

> miles of construction paper and wax crayon were expended. . . . As I inched sluggishly along the treadmill of the Maycomb County school system, I could not help receiving the impression that I was being cheated out of something. (pp. 32–33)

Cheated indeed—out of purposeful reading assignments, engaging dialogue, and writing instruction.

High-achieving Finland doesn't go in for such nonsense. After spending a year in a U.S. school, a Finnish student had to repeat the entire year when she returned to her home country. Instead of reading and writing, she had spent most of her time in her U.S. school on projects in which she was instructed to do things like "glue this to this poster for an hour" (Gamerman, 2008, p. 2).

Have we owned up to these shortcomings and their inevitable consequences? Is this the kind of education system educators and citizens really want for our kids? These activities are not peculiar to schools in less advantaged settings. They're a prominent K–12 phenomenon that does untold harm, especially to students in the early grades where reading levels are strongly predictive of lifelong literacy and career readiness.

One of the primary drivers of the Crayola curriculum is another ubiquitous, time-gobbling feature of K–3 literacy blocks: small-group instruction.

Small-Group Instruction: The Hidden Downsides

I've observed teachers working with a small group of students while the rest are working at centers, engaged in independent activities such as coloring. The teacher eventually works with five or six groups in a day. In a two-hour reading block, and with time spent transitioning between groups, each group receives about 20 minutes of actual instruction.

Starting in 1st grade, students need to spend the maximum amount of time learning the alphabetic code, reading, talking, and writing. However, we squander most of the reading block when we rely too much on small-group instruction. This arrangement has grown out of two misbegotten assumptions:

- That small-group teaching is more effective than whole-group instruction.
- That students are capable of learning to read and write on their own for extended periods.

The fact is, a heavy reliance on small-group instruction is not more but *less* effective than even typical (i.e., suboptimal) whole-group instruction (Sparks, 2018). Instead of narrowing gaps, such instruction widens reading gaps over time (Sparks, 2022). Small-group instruction is far less effective than sound, structured whole-class instruction, mostly because the latter multiplies the amount of precious, on-task learning time students receive.

To be clear, in an effective classroom, we wouldn't eliminate small groups; we would simply use them strategically and sparingly. Consider those five or six groups of students who get no more than 20 minutes of actual reading instruction each day. In a classroom where students receive effective whole-class teaching, they would easily receive about 80 minutes of teacher-led instruction. There's more time for intensive phonics, for reading, for learning general knowledge, for vocabulary lessons, for discussion, and for writing and writing instruction—for every student, every day (Schmoker, 2019a). In addition, it also leaves time for the teacher to spend additional time with students who need extra assistance.

This simple combination of (greatly) increased instructional time and effective whole-class teaching in the major elements of literacy is exceedingly effective. It can propel record proportions of students toward success in reading by the end of 3rd grade and beyond, and it can greatly narrow literacy gaps in middle and high school.

A major reason so many students don't become proficient readers in the early grades is quite simple. Except for the time when their group is with the teacher, they're engaged in a variety of unsupervised activities that make a limited contribution to their ability to read or write.

They often engage in these activities at centers or stations located around the classroom.

Literacy Centers—That Aren't

Among the most peculiar features of early-grade reading instruction is the prevalence of so-called literacy centers. They represent the triumph of convenience over rational action. They operate on the assumption that most students will learn to read, write, and acquire knowledge without much guidance or supervision.

Will they? Do learning centers and their attendant activities improve reading achievement? According to the studies, writes reading expert Timothy Shanahan (2018), the answer is no. He notes that time spent at such centers is, alas, "not a productive part of the school day" (p. 1). These centers consist mostly of the busywork I've described, such as what I saw when touring a school with abysmal reading scores. The school was on academic probation, but instead of teachers actually teaching students how to read and write, students were roving around the room, chatting quietly among stations, coloring, sorting objects or flashcards, operating tape recorders with headphones, or languidly turning the pages of a picture book, sometimes while gazing elsewhere.

In one classroom, students were cutting out small paper squares. Each contained an image representing a word with a consonant blend, for example "bl" and "tr." Students used crayons of different colors to carefully adorn each square while chatting with their partners. Then they applied paste to the back of each square and put the squares on a poster. This occupied them for most of the period, except for the short time each group had with the teacher.

Once again, we might blanch or despair at such practices, but we should instead consider what they reveal—a gold mine of productive time waiting to be repurposed to achieve unprecedented outcomes in literacy.

Test Prep: A Focus on Low-Level Skills

A bright, highly valued, second-year teacher—an Ivy League graduate— is teaching 1st graders in a school with a 100 percent poverty rate. She's teaching just five students at a time while the rest of the class works independently. These kids desperately need to learn the phonetic code; they need to read simple, content-rich text along with their teacher to build their vocabulary and knowledge base.

Instead, the teacher is teaching them, for the second time, how to identify and write captions. The concept is so abstract and boring that it eludes most of her students, but no matter. These students will continue, like millions of others, to be subjected to a daily diet of such bloodless skills. Teachers are trained to teach this way, even at Ivy League schools (Wexler, 2019).

I was recently asked to consult for a large metropolitan school district. Early on, they invited me to attend one of their monthly administrative meetings. That morning, all school administrators were being implored to raise reading scores by providing test-prep exercises focused on skills like inferencing, identifying cause and effect, and the notorious "finding the main idea." There was no mention in this long presentation about having students read or write more.

At the end of the meeting, I was asked to comment. I couldn't resist the chance to remind the audience of the research that decries such practices, which only supplant legitimate literacy instruction. The district afterward disinvited me to provide any additional consulting. I was reminded of an article by literacy expert Timothy Shanahan (2014). In it, he described how he became the object of a principal's disdainful glances when he encouraged her teachers to eschew test-prep exercises in favor of having students read and write.

We've known for decades that a focus on test-prep skills is a barrier to literacy, to students acquiring the ability to read and write. Author

and teacher Kelly Gallagher (2009) dubs such practices *readicide*—
the murder of reading. Not a single reading expert supports these
strategies as a way to help students become effective readers, writers,
or speakers.

Nevertheless, the focus on isolated skills is pervasive. I recently
toured a school that had received the state's lowest rating; most students struggled to read and decode. What did we find the students
doing? Circling prepositions in one class and completing a worksheet
on homonyms in another. Stanford's Sam Wineberg (2013) has been
similarly mystified when observing students—who could barely read—
being taught about assonance and alliteration.

These cases are not outliers. They are remarkably common and
help account for why many students arrive at college with good grades
but are "book virgins"—that is, they've never read an entire book (Lattier, 2016). Such students will reach adulthood only semiliterate. These
findings align with The New Teacher Project's (TNTP, 2018) estimate
that as many as 500 hours of time are wasted in school every year on
activities that don't contribute to academic or intellectual growth.
They don't only waste time; they're stupefyingly dull and sow cynicism
among students who endure these routines. On some level, most students know they're being cheated out of something.

Literacy isn't about coloring, cutting, test preparation, or skills
remediation. Once students can decode, it's all about abundant
amounts of "plain old reading and writing" at increasing levels of com-
plexity. As Annie Ward writes (2017), "We often diagnose deficits and
prescribe highly specialized treatments, without attending to the basic
proven remedy: a good book and time to read it" (p. 10).

Every study overwhelmingly demonstrates that when students
engage in ample amounts of meaningful, authentic reading, scores rise
commensurately. Predictably, various commercial programs claim to
promote these core activities. Not surprisingly, schools, habituated to
dependence on outside expertise, are happy to purchase them.

Buyer beware.

The Problem with Literacy Programs

For many years, elementary schools have taken a keen interest in popular reading curricula and programs, but mystery surrounds their content, use, and quality. As reading expert Mark Seidenberg points out, "These programs are put out by large publishers that aren't very forthcoming" about their content or effectiveness in classrooms (Seidenberg, cited in Schwartz, 2019, p. 1). Moreover, districts often accrete several programs, leaving teachers to select or combine their favorite elements from each. As Schwartz (2019) writes for *Education Week*, "There's no good way to peek into an elementary classroom to see what materials teachers are using" (p. 1).

Of course, all such curricula claim to be effective and research based. As a result, schools spend lavishly on them because billions of dollars in funding are available for their purchase. The most artfully marketed are the most popular, even though they aren't backed by science (Schwartz, 2019).

Aside from phonics programs, I've yet to come across a comprehensive early reading program I had faith in; the experts I most admire feel the same or have serious reservations about even their favorite programs. Some have told me they regard a select few programs as better than nothing—but only if heavily supplemented with additional reading and writing.

This is their most glaring weakness; even the highest-rated programs are light on "plain old reading and writing." That makes them inferior to the most straightforward, homegrown, teacher-generated English curricula instituted in the successful schools I'll describe at the end of this chapter.

These programs are unduly tainted by the very culture that brought us here—one inured to the harm done by worksheets, low-level discussions, and infrequent or watered-down reading and writing assignments. Publishers are savvy. They know that schools gravitate toward workbooks and worksheets and that these expensive items must be replenished annually. They're designed to produce a profit. In one rural Arizona elementary school, several of us carefully analyzed one of the most widely used programs. It was startlingly short on authentic literacy but long on trivial activities. We calculated that it would take almost twice the number of days in a school year to complete them all.

The executives from another popular K–12 reading program invited me to observe and endorse their program. Although it ostensibly stressed reading and writing, it was light on both and lacked the explicit, scaffolded instruction that enables students to comprehend grade-level texts. Moreover, it relied heavily on student-led, small-group discussions about books that students chose, all of this with little guidance from the teacher. Most of the groups we observed were off task until we came around to their tables. The quality of their discussions suffered from an absence of teacher guidance.

Even the program I most wanted to embrace was disappointing. Its research and philosophical base were unassailable, but the team that developed the actual product missed the mark (for reasons I'll share in a moment). Despite this, that program has benefitted greatly from strong endorsements from entities that rate such programs.

When the Ratings Go Awry

Several agencies, with good intentions, rate and curate elementary grade reading programs. How reliable are these ratings? Michael Goldstein (2020) contrasts such program evaluations to *Rotten Tomatoes* movie reviews and *Consumer Reports*. He points out that *Rotten Tomatoes* reviewers don't just read the script; they watch the movie. Likewise, if *Consumer Reports* looks at automobile quality, the reviewers don't just base their review on the appearance of the car or the manufacturer's claims but on their personal experiences driving the car. In other words, they test the product against performance metrics.

What prominent endorsers of literacy programs do is quite different. They base their ratings on survey data, not on evidence of effectiveness or the effect on student learning. This is hardly scientific;

although their tables and data arrays create a veneer of empiricism, they're misleading. They allow flawed programs to seemingly meet high program standards.

Consider my experience with one such program. It had just been given the highest across-the-board rating by one agency. However, when a group of us examined its materials, we saw problems. Despite some attractive features, the program was at odds with many of its originators' intentions. It gave excessive attention to phonics, well beyond grades K–1, which consumed time students should have been spending on reading and writing. It was heavy on worksheets and light on what the program's founder championed vigorously: reading entire, original works of literature as opposed to diluted adaptations and excerpts. Both writing and writing instruction were limited in the extreme.

Although the content orientation was admirable, the scripted lessons violated several core principles of effective instruction. For example, a sound lesson needs to have a single, clear objective and a corresponding assessment (Lemov, 2015; Marzano, 2007); more than one objective scatters focus and wreaks havoc on the lesson's effectiveness. Each lesson in this literacy program, however, contained multiple objectives, with no clear assessment of any of them. The lessons consisted of teacher talk and worksheets, and student participation in the discussions was voluntary. When we observed teachers using the program, we noticed a uniform pattern of teachers calling on that small, conscientious minority of students who raised their hands.

This is where it got interesting. On behalf of the district, I contacted the person who oversaw the development of the program. She confirmed our perceptions point by point and graciously admitted to her own frustrations—that the program had gotten away from the originators in the development stages. She conceded that it needed fundamental change. We were advised to ignore and replace much of the busywork and worksheets with far more reading and writing about authentic literature (Schmoker, 2019b).

Reading instruction in the elementary grades continues to fail us, but reading is only the first element of literacy. The ability to read empowers, and is empowered by, discussion and writing. All three cultivate the all-important abilities to think and effectively communicate our thoughts to others.

Before we examine the unfortunate state of secondary literacy, let's first examine the sobering state of discussion and writing at all levels K–12.

The Sad State of K–12 Discussion

In the main, we don't teach our students how to engage in meaningful discussions. We don't explicitly instruct them in how to articulate their thoughts with concision, clarity—and civility. Moreover, students rarely learn the importance of enunciating audibly, and they're seldom taught to listen carefully before responding to others' remarks. This prevents them from learning from their fellow students and from refining their thoughts and convictions. It deprives them of one of the richest sources of social and intellectual maturity: the chance to develop an informed, balanced disposition.

When I conduct classroom discussions as a visitor, I make sure students have read and processed the text so they'll have plenty to contribute. Then I liberally cold-call to ensure that all students participate. I gently coax them to speak loud enough so the class can hear them. Many need this coaxing (believe me). I also coach them to speak in fairly complete, comprehensible sentences. If their comments aren't clear, I encourage them to repeat or make their points differently. Their second attempts are always fruitful, both for themselves and their classmates. I also emphasize that we must respond to one another's remarks with the utmost civility.

Students enjoy these discussions immensely. For most, this is the first time a teacher has required them to participate in the discussion and the first time they have received instruction in, and constructive feedback on, these invaluable speaking skills and dispositions.

A few years ago, the education nonprofit Learning 24/7 conducted an in-house, informal study of about 1,500 classrooms. They found academic dialogue and discussion occurring in only 0.5 percent of the classrooms observed (Schmoker, 2006, p. 100). This is especially unfortunate when we consider that 83 percent of students identify "discussion and debate" as among their favorite ways to learn (Azzam, 2008).

Elmore (2005) found that genuine discussion is rare. When it does occur, it consists almost entirely of low-level questions. Likewise, Richard Allington (2001) found that school discussions operate on a recitation script of factual questions that only require quick, two- or three-word answers. In place of such "shallow and barren" exchanges, he chides us, substantive dialogue should be a daily experience (p. 88).

Two professors who have closely studied the current state of discussion in K–12 classrooms put it this way (Reznitskaya & Wilkinson, 2019):

> Studies from the past several decades consistently show that students in most classrooms rarely have the opportunity to participate in an open, extended, and intellectually rigorous exchange of ideas, during which they get to formulate and defend their own opinions and consider alternative propositions offered by their peers. This leaves most students unprepared for an information-dependent world in which they must engage and communicate with others as they sift through competing ideas and opinions. (p. 1)

This has dire consequences for democratic citizenship, which depends on rational, orderly deliberation to thrive. It has never been more important for students to have opportunities to listen carefully, weigh opposing views, and express their thoughts in a clear and respectful fashion. This is our best hedge against the intolerance and extremism we see so much of today. As Jennifer Frey (2021) writes, "Civility," as learned through the respectful exchange of ideas, "is the most basic and obvious virtue to be taught in our public schools." This is crucial because according to David Brooks (2022), members of a democracy "are not born, they are made":

> We need to fortify the institutions that are supposed to teach the democratic skills: how to weigh evidence and commit to truth; how

to correct for your own partisan blinders and learn to doubt your own opinions; how to respect people you disagree with; how to avoid catastrophism, conspiracy, and apocalyptic thinking; how to avoid supporting demagogues; how to craft complex compromises. (Brooks, 2022, para. 28)

Our failure to place such civil, intellectual discourse at the heart of the K–12 curriculum is apparent in our universities. Northwestern University professors Morson and Schapiro (2021) report that high school graduates, more than ever, are arriving at college "eager to demonize their colleagues over political differences and to shun or shame people for transgressions." Rather than wanting to expand their intellectual horizons, they arrive "remarkably confident in their views on nearly everything" (para. 4).

In Morson's and Schapiro's hugely popular course, students feel safe as they listen to one another's strongest arguments and "consider that they might just be wrong" in some of their views. The professors add that all educators "must be mindful that genuine dialogue is the lifeblood of democracy, requiring an unending exchange—and testing—of ideas" and of the "ideological fashions" that surround us (Morson & Schapiro, 2021, para. 13).

Such courses should be the model for K–12 education as it seeks to redress the near-absence of intellectually oriented discussion grounded in subject-area content. (See Schmoker, 2018, for questions and question stems for literature and nonfiction in each of the core disciplines.)

What of the general state of writing and writing instruction?

The Even Sadder State of Writing

Writing is far more than an isolated skill. It's the "litmus test of thought"—an activity with a "miraculous power" to promote students' ability to retain, analyze, process, and synthesize what they read (Conley, 2007, p. 23). It's among the most sought-after professional skills and possibly the most important skill for college readiness. For all this, writing and writing instruction are among the most infrequent activities you'll find in schools. The negative effect on college and career readiness is palpable (Conley, 2005; Varlas, 2016).

My oldest daughter attended an award-winning, top-10 elementary school in our metropolitan area. On her first report card, she received an *A* in English. At the first parent-teacher conference, we asked the teacher about our daughter's writing. She was caught off guard. All she could tell us was that our daughter's writing "was fine." When we probed to find out what she meant by "fine," she became flustered. I then asked if she happened to have any record of writing assignments in her grade book or if she might be able to describe some—any—of these assignments. She was unprepared for such questions. I begged off.

Two years later, we inquired why our daughter didn't appear to have been given any writing assignments by late October. The teacher told us that she hadn't gotten around to teaching writing that year because someone had loaned her a class set of microscopes, which had occupied the students for several weeks. We couldn't see how this prevented her from teaching or assigning writing in English.

I eventually met with the principal. She told me she had no idea whether or how frequently students wrote in their classrooms. While there, I showed her a handbook describing the grade-level writing requirements issued by the state. She'd never seen it and asked if she could borrow it. No changes ensued, so we continued, as we always had, to teach our children how to write on our own time at home. That principal went on to become the district's assistant superintendent—of curriculum and instruction.

I later consulted, pro bono, for that district's highest-poverty, lowest-scoring school. In a grade-level meeting, I asked the team about writing. The team members looked at one another confusedly until one of them said they hadn't gotten around to it yet (it was spring). Another one said they hadn't been trained to teach writing. In fact, writing researchers have known for decades that little or no writing instruction takes place in regular classrooms (Kameenui & Carnine, 1998).

Education professor Robert Reid (cited in Harris et al., 2008) delivers this stark assessment: Anyone who has "worked in our schools for long is well aware that there is a problem with written expression in this country. Put simply, our kids don't know how to write. . . . They've never been taught how to write" (p. ix).

We might hope that writing instruction increases in the secondary years. It doesn't. To make this point, Darling-Hammond (2010) cites a revealing passage from Tom Wolfe's *The Bonfire of the Vanities* (1987). A parent asks the headmaster of a pricey private prep school why his son does so little writing. The headmaster "let out a whoop" and then informed the man that they hadn't taught writing in "fifteen years! Maybe twenty!" (Wolfe, p. 228). Wolfe wrote that book 35 years ago.

Ultimately, we may misunderstand the term *writing instruction* altogether. George Hillocks (1987) is among the pioneers of meta-analytic studies in education; his specialty is writing research. He found that an average writing lesson in K–12 schools lasts only three minutes. This can hardly be termed "instruction" in any meaningful sense.

Sean Connors is among the most effective high school writing teachers I've observed. I was in his class the day his students told him that until they took his class, they had received almost no instruction in expository or persuasive writing.

Think about that.

In an article in *USA Today* (Harrington-Lueker, 2002), the writer laments the way arts and crafts projects have supplanted writing assignments in particular:

> Talk to teachers, review messages posted on e-mail groups, and browse professional journals, and you'll find high school assignments that are long on fun and remarkably short on actual writing.
>
> For example, someone who teaches an honors class for high school freshmen posts a short-story project that allows students 13 options, including: create a map to illustrate the story's setting, make a game to show the story's theme, put together a collage from magazine photographs, or assemble a scrapbook or photograph album for the character. . . . Have your students design a coat of arms . . . draw the design for a book jacket. (p. A-13)

These activities, the author writes, may entertain some students, but the fallout is predictable. Students leave high school with severely stunted expressive abilities, and they're showing up at college unable to write.

Truth—And the Consequences

The effect of this dereliction is broad. When I taught college English, most of my students arrived with limited writing skills. In 1995, NAEP asked high schools to submit the very best papers from their most talented student writers. The samples revealed that even "the best [writing] is mediocre" (Olson, 1995, p. 5); fully 43 percent of the samples received a "low" rating.

Faculty at elite, Ivy league colleges agree. They can't understand why students with excellent GPAs write less effectively than ever (Bartlett, 2003). David Conley (2007) found that writing ability is the single most widespread, crippling deficit among entering college students.

There has been no systemwide improvement in either writing or writing instruction over the years. NAEP scores have not improved. Many report a serious decline in writing skills, even in the Common Core era (Gallagher, 2017; Hirsch, 2016; Wexler, 2019).

This parallels corporate recruiters' complaints that "the biggest skill that people are missing is the ability to communicate" in both written and oral formats (Wagner, 2008). This is painfully apparent in the "mangled language" of typical business communications, written by people with college degrees (Bermudez, 2016).

This has real-world consequences. According to *The New York Times* (Dillon, 2004), the one thing "corporate America can't build [is] a sentence" (p. 1). About one-third of employees in blue chip companies write so poorly that they must undergo remedial training in how to clarify their thoughts to colleagues and customers.

In view of this urgent need, the recent call by some theorists to *reduce* the time and emphasis given to writing in schools is dispiriting. This won't help poor students or students of color; it will hold them back. For *The New York Times* columnist Michelle Goldberg (2021), this denigration of writing and the written word, now included in some administrative training, is "ridiculous and harmful" to students; for Bergner (2021), it would leave students less ready for college and competition in the labor market.

Writing and writing instruction deserve far *more* time and attention than they now receive. Writing is still, as a landmark study proclaims (National Commission on Writing, 2003), the neglected *R*.

Let's now focus on overall literacy instruction at the secondary level—and on the preponderance of "stuff."

Secondary Literacy: The Triumph of "Stuff"

I'm fond of Richard Allington's (2001) useful phrase—the "reading and writing vs. 'stuff' ratio" (p. 8). Genuine literacy continues to be crowded out by the ever-present "stuff" that has no business in classrooms.

After my article "The Crayola Curriculum" appeared in *Education Week*, I received an email from Carol Jago, a veteran high school teacher and then president of the National Council of Teachers of English. She pointed out that coloring was not only a feature of elementary literacy; it was also rife at the secondary level.

Author and consultant Ruth Mitchell (2004) encountered plenty of "stuff" in the high school classrooms she visited. Instead of reading and writing, students were drawing and coloring shields representing Greek gods and goddesses. Award-winning writer and education professor Lisa Delpit (2012) found high school students coloring turkeys with different colored pens. I shouldn't have been surprised. One of my own high school English instructors had us spend whole periods drawing pictures of our favorite characters from Stephen Crane's *The Red Badge of Courage* and other novels.

As I began to visit high school classrooms, I discovered a teacher whose students spent an entire week making elaborate posters, in groups, on the "elements of fiction" (e.g., rising action, conflict, setting). Her class looked like an art studio with paint, markers, poster paper, and glitter scattered everywhere. Each team then made a presentation to the class. I asked the teacher how this contributed to literacy. With deep conviction, she told me that concepts were important and that building these posters helped students internalize them.

There is no support—zero—for such inanity. If we began to replace such "stuff" with purposeful reading, dialogue, and writing, the effect would be momentous.

You might think these stories are exaggerated. They aren't. When my daughter attended a charter secondary school that had good test scores, we again noticed that she wasn't doing much reading or writing. This school branded itself as a place where students would learn to write and be prepared for college. However, from the way my daughter described it, her honors English course sounded more like a drama class. So I called the teacher. She informed me, without any embarrassment, that because honors students were under such pressure these days and had so much work to do, her entire, yearlong curriculum consisted of having her students perform skits and complete a 25-poem portfolio.

When I shared this with the principal, it was news to him. With a little probing, he discovered that none of the English teachers in the school taught writing, although one excellent social studies teacher made writing a meaningful part of her curriculum. The principal wasn't aware of that either, affirming Richard Elmore's (1999–2000) finding that most principals are neither trained in, nor inclined toward, managing either what or how well anything gets taught.

So we switched schools—and got equally frustrating results. In one daughter's English class, students were asked to create any one of the following to demonstrate their understanding of a novel:

- A diorama
- An illustrated map
- A book jacket
- A movie poster
- A 3D mobile

There was no writing option.

Another teacher had students spend much of the semester creating a bulging "literary scrapbook" in which students kept artwork and drawings of their favorite characters and scenes. Students spent days combing through magazines to find art and photos to create collages in response to the minimal number of readings they completed that year.

Let's look at some other forms of "stuff" that hide from education's rightful stakeholders—and perhaps from the conscious awareness of educators themselves.

Slideshows, Movies, and Worksheets (Oh My!)

I did some extensive consulting at an award-winning school where a team of teachers had decided to blend two subject areas (English and social studies). Given the typically ill-defined curricular parameters for these core courses, this attempt at interdisciplinary education devolved into a series of unfocused group slideshow projects. There were no writing assignments. One or two members of each student group did most of the presenting, while the rest of the team chimed in with an occasional sentence or two. The rest of the class simply sat idly through the presentations, which lasted for several days. The teachers lavishly praised the presentations, and all students received high grades.

More recently, I was in line at a coffee shop behind two students who attended the highest-scoring high school in the area. They were speaking animatedly about their English teachers, so I offered to buy their coffee if I could pick their brains for a few minutes. Fortunately, both students had brought folders from their respective English courses. They were stuffed with worksheets and only a few short writing assignments. I asked them if they had written anything longer that year (it was late spring). They hadn't.

They also told me that the teacher had assigned only three books that year. One of the students mumbled something about Homer's *The Odyssey*. When I asked whether they'd read the epic, they replied no, they had watched a movie *based* on it—the Coen Brothers' *Oh Brother, Where Art Thou?* I was reminded of how one of my daughter's teachers had included a Shakespeare play in her syllabus, *The Taming of the Shrew*. The students ended up spending three days watching a movie instead—*Ten Things I Hate About You* (which is loosely based on that play).

You can't make this stuff up. It reflects the slow, unnoticed erosion of literacy standards and expectations over the decades.

Low Expectations for Literacy

At one of the high schools where I taught English, I was assigned classes for the lowest-performing students, as new faculty often are. When I asked what books were available, I was informed that these kids couldn't be expected to read books. For years, the mainstay of their curriculum had been a slick, heavily illustrated student magazine with short articles, games, and crossword puzzles. I asked my department head if I could reappropriate my budget for several novels. He was delighted—and surprised to discover that I was teaching these students how to write expository papers about Steinbeck novels, which they enjoyed.

The use of low-level teaching materials is in keeping with the downward drift in expectations for English and literacy; it's the fruit of prominent theories that discouraged educators from assigning challenging work to students. The reigning assumption became this: Assigned readings must be within students' "comfort levels." In practice, those levels kept moving in the direction of the lowest-achieving students. As I've noted, only 17 percent of reading and writing assignments are grade-level appropriate; the percentage is even lower for poor and marginalized populations (TNTP, 2018). This downward spiral is, in part, a consequence of a lack of teacher training in evidence-based teaching methods that enable students to learn both faster and at much higher levels of challenge.

Expectations are low in writing even in well-to-do zip codes. Sheryl Sandberg, the COO of Facebook through 2022, attended a high-scoring high school in an affluent area. She was shocked at how poorly that school prepared her for college-level writing; in four years of high school, she wrote only one five-page paper. Sandberg suddenly found herself in college where she "had to write five-page papers overnight" in multiple courses (Alter, 2014, p. 72).

Exclusive private schools, too, have succumbed to curricular literary chaos. Two prominent writers recently pulled their child out of such a school, which had, at one time, maintained high literacy expectations (Riley, 2020b). However, it had become a place where students read few books, and writing assignments were rare.

I was once asked to evaluate instruction at the most exclusive private school in a large metropolitan area. The campus buildings resembled something out of Harry Potter. Student uniforms were stunning. Male teachers wore tweed; some even wore bow ties. Nevertheless, in classroom after classroom, most of what I saw was the same feeble, ineffective teaching—as well as worksheets. The frustrated headmaster and I saw no writing and no meaningful discussions.

The gradual collapse of literacy standards creates what we have today: a gaping mismatch between K–12 experience and college preparation, between K–12 experiences and the demands of careers and responsible citizenship. Whether students attend college or not, this failure denies them the rich intellectual and career benefits of learning to write well.

The Common Core: A "Nothingburger"

The English language arts Common Core State Standards were intended to redress this drift. Its failure points to the current system's capacity to bend even the most well-intended efforts against its ostensible goals. Surely, we would think, a decade-long, massively funded national effort to carefully define and promote effective literacy instruction would have some payoff. It didn't.

The Common Core project started out full of promise, with a research-based call for a return to the fundamental elements of literacy. Had it stayed faithful to that goal, it would have fulfilled its purpose—to facilitate the development of high-quality, literacy-rich curricula across the subject areas. It would have resulted in historic increases in the amount of time students spent on purposeful reading, writing, and discussion.

It had no such effect. The lead team's solid initial work was turned over to myriad committees, which then converted it into an exhaustive, jargon-laced taxonomy of grade-by-grade skills and minutiae. The state assessments that emerged from their work do indeed give us a more accurate picture of students' literacy skills. We can be thankful for that. The standards themselves, though, are worse than most of the state-level documents they were supposed to improve on—so much so that the initial architects of the Common Core distanced themselves from the final published version.

As misbegotten as the standards were, training in them became an industry, consuming the lion's share of professional development time and money. After 10 years of unprecedented amounts of presentations and (so-called) training, the American Institute for Research (Loveless, 2020) found that the standards hadn't improved student literacy. Scores went down, not up, during the Common Core era. In the end, writes Rick Hess (2021b), "The whole thing was a big nothingburger" (p. 1).

This is how the current K–12 system operates. It launches initiatives to address a problem, and then it develops solutions that enable it to maintain the status quo. This sad cycle is sustained by ignorance—and by trust in a system that has learned to create the appearance of improvement effort without addressing two vital elements:

- Legitimate (as opposed to token or misguided) training.
- Competent instructional management.

Without these, even the most well-funded initiative will eventually amount to "a big nothingburger." This and more hides within the black box of literacy instruction in schools and classrooms.

Literacy Problems—Opportunities in Disguise

Before we look at schools that have taken action to achieve "stunningly powerful consequences" in literacy instruction, let's review some of the brutal facts of current practice. These point to rich, ripe opportunities for improvements in literacy:

- In the crucial primary years, about two-thirds of the long morning literacy block is spent on coloring, pasting, and related activities.
- Only a minority of U.S. teachers provides systematic, intensive phonics instruction.
- Small-group instruction dominates early-grade literacy instruction, even though it is less effective than whole-group instruction and greatly reduces instructional time.
- Only about 17 percent of school reading assignments are at students' grade level.
- The use of off-grade materials; worksheets; and arts, crafts, and related activities accounts for about 500 unproductive classroom hours each year.
- Rational, civil discussion is at the heart of civic and communal life and of democratic governance, yet it's seldom taught and practiced in our schools.
- Despite the outsize importance of writing to college and career success, students seldom write and are rarely taught to write effectively.

Hundreds of hours are waiting to be turned to fairly traditional educational activities that have vastly higher yields in terms of student learning. Teachers could implement most of these activities within weeks, others as soon as tomorrow morning. We could all be celebrating the student benefits of this shift within a school year, as the following cases demonstrate.

What Effective Literacy Instruction Looks Like

I've studied and visited a variety of schools whose exceptional gains in literacy attest to the power of the most obvious, effective literacy instruction. The success of these schools also attests to the power of curriculum. In each of these cases, teachers deliberately integrated reading, discussion, and writing assignments into the weekly fabric of English, social studies, science, and other courses.

In a Tucson-area school district where I worked, two 1st grade teachers team-taught to provide large amounts of mostly whole-class phonics instruction. They paired this with read-alouds, read-alongs, and generous opportunities for students to write. Students did no coloring, cutting, or pasting during the reading block. As a result, more than 90 percent of the students at this high-poverty school could read at grade level by the end of 1st grade.

A few years back, I visited Bessemer Elementary School, which is located in a rural, high-poverty community in Colorado. The school's reading and writing scores were deplorable—until a no-nonsense superintendent, Joyce Bales, arrived. She called out the coloring she was seeing in classrooms. Under her guidance, student pass rates on the state assessment rose from 12 to 64 percent in reading and from 2 to 48 percent in writing. In two years.

Christy Moore, a literacy coach in Indiana, saw me present research on the need to greatly increase the amount of time students spend reading, discussing, and writing during the school day. She persuaded her K–3 faculty to go all-in on these activities. Here's a portion of her email to me describing their first-year effort:

> I want you to know that the students in our building can read, discuss (debate), and write across all grade levels . . . the voracious reading and discussion have caused our students to grow at accelerated levels. Our students now read for 60–90 minutes a day and write for at least

45 minutes. Even our youngest don't want to leave the discussion group, even when it spills over into their specials time.

Our scores are proving it. In 3rd grade, we went from only 59 percent passing our state assessment last year (we haven't been out of the 60s in more than 10 years) to an amazing 82 percent! In our model classrooms, where I spent more time training and modeling, the students passed at a rate of 98 percent.

When I lived in Colorado, I was invited to visit a school in the Poudre Valley to learn about the results they were getting with special education students. They had abandoned typical approaches and arranged, instead, for students to spend most of their class time reading and talking about what they read, every single day. This was remarkable: The reading diet of special education students is ordinarily reduced from the moment they're categorized, but with this approach, the special education students made an average gain of two years in reading every year. After two years, the majority were able to leave special education altogether.

In another district where I worked, special education teacher Linda Quieruga adopted a similar approach in her high school. Whenever I visited her class, students were either reading or writing, almost from bell to bell. Her high school students made average gains of more than two years in a single semester; a few made three-year gains.

In that same district, two teachers at La Cima Middle School revamped their English and social studies courses. They began to provide students with a near-daily diet of close reading, annotating, discussion, and writing about literary and historical texts. Students wrote an argumentative essay about the issues in their texts every week. In one year, at a school with a 50 percent free and reduced-price lunch rate, student scores rose from the state average to a three-way tie for first place; the two schools they tied with were both situated in one of the most affluent zip codes in the state.

In the previous chapter, I mentioned the accomplishments of Mead Valley Elementary School in California, a school with a 95 percent poverty rate. What I didn't mention was that their curriculum was literacy rich; all students read common grade-level texts and wrote daily. For each grading period, teachers established clear, common expectations for the length and quality of writing assignments. For example, by 5th grade, all students would be able to write a sound, five-paragraph document. (Schmoker, 2020, makes the case for such grade-level curricular standards for writing.)

Of course, those who embraced the Crayola curriculum at the school resisted such measures, but Mead Valley's principal put an end to that. "We love the arts," he said, "but we don't do arts and crafts during sacred literacy time" (Reeves, 2007, p. 2). The school made measurable improvements on state assessments in the first year; in the next few years, the school's Academic Performance Index (API) for reading and math rose dramatically—from 450 to 774, on par with wealthy suburban schools.

New Dorp High School, in New York City, was failing so badly in English that it was targeted for closure. More than anything, according to *The Atlantic*'s Peg Tyre (2012), students lacked the ability to express themselves effectively. They were unable to "translate thoughts into coherent, well-argued sentences, paragraphs, and essays" (para. 3). With the help of a skilled consultant, the faculty learned to teach students how to speak clearly and logically in class discussions. Teachers combined this with an intense focus on frequent analytic, expository writing about the content students were reading and learning in their core courses.

The drivers of this approach were fully aware that it represented a "dramatic departure from what most American students—especially low performers—are taught in school" (Tyre, 2012, para. 4). Because it raised expectations, it met early resistance; most New Dorp faculty thought that marginalized students were simply not smart enough to write well. That changed when these strategies yielded extraordinary results. Within a single year, New Dorp students were scoring higher on exams than any previous class. In two years, the success rate on the challenging English Regents exam rose from 67 to 89 percent. The number of students who had to take remedial courses in English—to earn a diploma—shrank from 175 to 40. The graduation rate rose from 63 to 80 percent. In a three-year period, students taking college-level classes increased from 148 to 412. As Tyre noted, New Dorp kids were learning, for the first time, how to "listen to each other, think more carefully, and speak more precisely, in ways that could then echo in persuasive writing" (Tyre, 2012, para. 34).

Brockton High School's commitment to reading, writing, speaking, and reasoning was built directly into the curriculum, every week in every course, at this large (more than 4,000 students) high-poverty school in Massachusetts. In every course, students read and wrote in the expository, interpretive, and argumentative modes and received explicit writing instruction. Teachers regularly collected and analyzed samples of student writing for improvement purposes. Their literacy-rich curriculum was the primary reason Brockton made the largest gains in the state during the first year of the effort. In the next five years, the school rose from bottom-dweller to the top 10 percent of schools in terms of achievement on the challenging Massachusetts Comprehensive Assessment System (MCAS) exam (Ferguson, 2016; Susan Szachowicz, personal communication).

Like Brockton High, View Park Preparatory High School in South Los Angeles, California, developed a coherent, guaranteed English language arts curriculum that began with a simple regimen: each month, students wrote two argumentative papers. Writing assignments were preceded by close reading of one or more texts in response to a guiding question, which drove the analytic and intellectually rich Socratic discussions that followed. This was so successful in English and history that the school incorporated argumentative writing into all disciplines. Teachers at View Park speak of how students gain immeasurably from just one year at the school; by the end of 9th grade, students have already become confident writers who are "prepared to write in college and to think through and logically argue their points in multiple disciplines" (Hernandez, Kaplan, & Schwartz, 2006, p. 50)

When this routine was instituted, View Park, whose student body is 97 percent Black, rose to be the highest-achieving majority-minority school in California (Hernandez, Kaplan, & Schwartz, 2006). Ninety percent of the school's 2008 graduates were accepted into four-year colleges (Landsberg, 2008).

These secondary school examples resemble a literacy-rich curriculum for 5th graders I saw in a high-poverty school in East Los Angeles. On most Fridays, the teacher taught his students how to write an essay. That's about 30 essays each year on such argumentative questions and prompts as "Weigh in on George's decision to kill Lennie in Steinbeck's *Of Mice and Men*." In a school with a 90 percent economically disadvantaged population, these students typically performed above the 90th percentile on state tests.

Make no mistake: Writing raises test scores.

I recently spoke with Jesse Sanchez, principal at Brawley Union High School in California. Students of color make up 90 percent of the student body, and the school has a 75 percent free and reduced-price lunch rate. One day, Sanchez found himself reading samples of student writing. "What I was reading," he said, "wasn't making any sense" (in Harrington, 2018). It worried him that his kids lacked the ability to make and support arguments, so he persuaded faculty to have students write every week about their reading, using a template for argumentative and expository writing. Students learned to cite sources and marshal evidence in every class, including physical education, where they wrote about topics such as muscle anatomy and weight training.

Like Brockton and View Park, the new regimen had an effect during the very first year. In three years, scores rose from 32 percent of students meeting or exceeding the standard on the new, more challenging state tests in English language arts, to 64 percent—at a time when overall state scores went down, not up. This focus on writing had an effect in math as well; three times as many students could now pass the state exam. This put Brawley Union in the top 25 schools in California in terms of the most rapid academic growth (Harrington, 2018).

Sanchez recently told me that more than 70 percent of his students now succeed on these much tougher state exams.

It's important to note that in all the cases I've cited, simply having students write every week about subject-area content caused learning levels and test scores to surge.

I met Sean Connors, an English teacher who taught in the community where I lived, when his principal invited me to observe one of Connors's lessons. Connors's preferred technology was a whiteboard and an overhead projector. His students didn't watch movies; they didn't color or make posters or scrapbooks. They read and wrote and read and wrote. In his first year at the school, the performance of his students alone caused aggregate scores at his high school to make the largest writing gains in the state. That is what can happen when we repurpose the hundreds of hours currently spent on "stuff" and focus them on meaningful literacy instruction.

Let me repeat. The absence of a coherent, literacy-rich curriculum and the most fundamental literacy practices underscores a gargantuan opportunity for dramatic school improvement. These two pivotal aspects of schooling afford tremendous room for growth and improvement because they're so rarely found in our schools.

Once a school has established such a curriculum, the greatest growth will come from how teachers deliver it. If we wish to optimize the effect of coherent curriculum and authentic literacy, then sound, structured instruction is key. That will be the topic of the next chapter.

How to Manage a Schoolwide Focus on Literacy: Action Questions for Leaders

- Have you conducted an audit of the actual, taught curriculum at your school to determine how much "stuff" supplants and intrudes on genuine literacy activities, such as explicit phonics instruction and purposeful reading, discussion, and writing?
- For the early grades in your school, have you developed a plan to *reduce* the amount of small-group instruction and *increase*

whole-group teaching to double or triple the amount of reading instruction students receive?

- Is your curriculum literacy rich? Are teachers building an ample, course-appropriate number of reading, discussion, and writing assignments into weekly coursework in every discipline? (See Schmoker, 2020, for guidance on this.)
- Have you provided professional development (reinforced through the work of professional learning communities) on how to
  — Provide scaffolded instruction that shows students how to analyze text?
  — Conduct engaging, open-ended, text-based discussions in which all students participate?
  — Teach basic elements of writing? These would include how to write a claim, how to identify and underline or annotate textual evidence, how to integrate quoted or paraphrased material, and how to support a claim with evidence and reasoning. (See Schmoker, 2018, pp. 100–112, for detailed guidance.)

4

Effective Instruction:
A Remarkable Convergence

*Improvement takes recognition of and
moral outrage at ineffective practices.*

—Roland Barth, Harvard Graduate School of Education

The evidence for the basic elements of explicit or structured teaching has a formidable pedigree. Its near disuse in schools is among the most baffling features of schooling, since its basic moves derive from timeless principles of learning. The language that describes it has been adopted, happily, by numerous researchers, which attests to the strong degree of agreement on its basic DNA.

Structured Teaching

I borrow the helpful term *structured teaching* from Douglas Fisher and Nancy Frey (2007), who have done excellent work in advancing its basic concepts. It's sometimes referred to as *explicit* or *scaffolded* instruction. The model incorporates certain basic, widely agreed-on elements of instruction that stress the gradual release of responsibility from teacher to student (Pearson & Gallagher, 1983). Significantly, structured teaching equips students for less structured activities; it enables them to continue the learning on their own and complete complex projects and assignments independently (Schmoker, 2018; Seidenberg, 2017).

We can incorporate numerous helpful methods into an effective lesson (Lemov, 2015), but let's look at a few primary elements first because they do the most to ensure that the greatest number of students will succeed on daily lessons.

Reduced to their essence, the most effective lessons are those in which students are given a **clear aim** or **objective**, linked to a corresponding **assessment** for what they're supposed to learn. For example, "I will be able to solve equations with two variables" or "I will be able to write a coherent paragraph to support a claim with textual evidence." By itself, a clear, focused objective and assessment greatly increase the student success rate on any daily lesson (Hattie, 2009; Marzano, 2007).

To ensure that students achieve the objective, the teacher **models** or instructs in small, **manageable steps or chunks** at a reasonably brisk pace. Following each step, students attempt or apply what was modeled, often working in pairs (**guided practice**) as the teacher **checks for understanding** to see if they're struggling or need additional instruction. If so, the teacher must break learning down into smaller chunks or **reteach** to target student confusion and thus promote every student's success on every phase of that day's lesson.

Such active and interactive scaffolded teaching has an indisputable effect on learning for all students, especially struggling students. Moreover, it powerfully fosters attentiveness, focused effort, and confidence because it promotes success at every stage of the lesson for the highest possible proportion of students. It's so effective that it can compensate for significant gaps in ability and background. In some cases, the success rate on daily lessons can approach 100 percent (Bornstein, 2011). That's why Robert Marzano (2007) encourages teachers to make these basic elements routine components of every lesson. At certain stages of learning, they are crucial to student success, from basic skills to the most sophisticated tasks.

To those who still contend that students learn better on their own without such structure, instructional expert David Bornstein (2011) has a compelling response: "Asking children to make their own discoveries before they solidify the basics is like asking them to compose songs on the guitar before they can form a C chord" (para. 6). Such lessons need not be perfect or particularly creative. My observations confirm the work of those who have found that the most effective lessons are "as plain vanilla as could be imagined" (Goodwin, 2011, p. 135). They are typically "mundane, unremarkable," even "disappointing" to those who expect them to be complex or "innovative" (Lemov, 2015, p. 10). This is encouraging. It means that any teacher trained to deliver such teaching can implement it successfully.

The world-class success of Finland's schools speaks to this. A U.S. teacher taught there for a full school year and was surprised to discover that their methods are anything but cutting edge—Finnish teachers typically employ teacher-directed classroom instruction (Stoltzfus, 2017), which Americans and their education schools so often decry.

How strong is the evidence base for such instruction? As strong as anything we know about effective schooling.

The Case for Structured Teaching

It's hard to overstate the case for structured teaching. Eminent researchers around the world have pled for its implementation for half a century.

In the 1960s, UCLA's Madeline Hunter helped clarify and codify such instruction. Her influence was seminal. Her terms, such as *checking for understanding,* are still commonly employed. One of her students, James Popham (2008), helped cement her reputation by finding that the gains from such instruction were among the largest ever reported.

Other prominent voices have weighed in on the power of explicit, step-by-step, whole-class instruction: Marilyn Burns, John Hattie,

Barack Rosenshine, Robert Marzano, Paul Kirschner, Dylan Wiliam, and dozens of others (Schmoker, 2018). Wiliam (2007) found that such instruction could double or triple the rate at which students acquire knowledge and skill every year. It could accelerate the speed of learning by a factor of four.

Multiple researchers found that the most effective instruction is typically *frontal*—taught to the entire class from the front of the room, as opposed to working with small groups of students. Between each small step of the lesson, it's supremely important that teachers (1) quickly circulate to observe a sample of students to gauge their progress—or patterns of struggle (checking for understanding). If students need additional help, effective teachers don't rush frantically from student to student trying to tutor each one. Instead, they (2) succinctly reteach the entire class to address those patterns—for each step—until the lesson is completed (Rosenshine, 2012).

When two bestselling journalists went looking for the best teaching in the world, they discovered wide, international agreement on this basic approach. *The Atlantic's* Amanda Ripley visited the highest achieving, most-improved school systems on the planet. She found that these countries' best teachers assiduously applied checks for understanding in their teaching, something she knew nothing about before her research. In her bestseller *The Smartest Kids in the World* (2013), she writes that this constituted the most stunning finding to come out of education in the past decade. It's actually among the most stunning findings of the last *several* decades.

Education writer Elizabeth Green (2014) made the same discovery. In *Building a Better Teacher*, she, too, found that the best teachers taught the entire class in small steps while monitoring progress—again, checking for understanding between each step and then reteaching those steps where students struggled. Then there's Doug Lemov, who features prominently in Green's book. His reputation derives primarily from his book *Teach Like a Champion* (2010), which is a highly practical guide to explicit, scaffolded instruction.

In the second edition, *Teach Like a Champion 2.0*, Lemov (2015) amps up what he found to be the pivotal element in good instruction—again, checking for understanding. He devotes the first two long chapters to the concept. He found that checking for understanding accounts, more than any other element, for the stunning success of the best teachers in his hugely successful network of charter schools (whose accomplishments we'll learn about in a moment).

Finally, there's Charles Payne (2007), who studied successful, diverse, urban schools. He reserves special praise for one method that accounts for what he refers to as "whopping improvements" (p. 95) in the most challenging, underserved schools: continuous, formative checks for understanding, followed by adjustments to instruction.

As we'll see, few education professors will deny the power of such teaching for a meaningful portion of the curriculum. Nevertheless, schools of education do little to impart this knowledge to prospective teachers or to train them to execute such instruction. We'll explore the reasons for this in Chapter 6.

To supercharge the quality of such instruction, I would love to see enterprising schools experiment with a four-period workday. This would provide a significant fund of time for teachers to collaborate, share, plan, and refine lessons together. It would increase their daily reserves of energy, which benefits highly effective teaching. In countries such as Finland, Japan, Germany, China, and France, teachers actually teach for fewer hours each week than their U.S. counterparts (Darling-Hammond, 2020). In many cases, such schedules have been achieved with a combination of creative scheduling and adjustments to class size. Such a model would address the urgent need to improve teacher morale.

Explicit, structured teaching is so powerful that it obviates the need for more cumbersome remediation or tutorial programs. When students receive effective instruction, it often eliminates the need for such supports (Vanderheyden et al., 2016). Despite all this, such high-leverage, structured instruction seldom occurs in most schools.

The End of Instruction

I was once asked to visit classrooms—along with the principal and some central office staff—in the only A+ school in an urban, high-poverty district. They wanted to showcase their best teachers. In the six or so classrooms we observed, we didn't see a single actual lesson. We did see teachers assigning tasks or distributing worksheets, with brief directions, to their students. We saw some teachers alternating between sitting at their desks and roaming the classroom to assist or prod individual students to do their work; some students only worked when thus coaxed. Some teachers would attempt to tutor one struggling student at a time while the rest of the class, confused by the assignment, shouted for help or waited for their turn, which never came for most of them before the period ended. Although I've witnessed this routine countless times, the group was convinced that what we saw was an anomaly. To follow up, two principals each identified and invited their most effective teacher to provide us with a partial sample of a lesson of their choosing. We told the teachers to treat us exactly like students, as though the information were brand new to us.

Within minutes, it became apparent that the teachers had never learned the rudiments of structured teaching. Both were charming and articulate, but neither clarified the objective of the lesson. Both covered several difficult steps without pausing, making no attempt to check for our understanding at all. Each teacher asked questions along the way but then called on whoever raised their hand first. When they got a correct answer, they immediately moved on, without circulating and without making any effort to find out if the rest of us were keeping up.

First one administrator, then another gently hinted to one of the teachers that she needed to instruct us in small steps, then give us opportunities to practice while she circulated to check our progress. All of this was plainly new to her. The session ended in tears.

You had to feel for her. She was talented and enthusiastic, but although she seemed familiar with the language of good instruction—most teachers are—she had never been adequately trained in, coached in, or evaluated on her mastery of these essential moves.

I once toured a school in New England with its leadership team. In one class, 10 minutes into the period, students were still walking around chatting while the teacher roved around, passing out worksheets and shouting sporadic directions above the din. Students loudly interrupted her several times to ask random questions, which she responded to. The leadership team later told me this was one of their best teachers.

This teacher deserved better. She deserved better university preparation, better professional development, and better instructional management than she had received.

These tendencies are depressingly common in both low- and high-performing schools. As far as the latter is concerned, their relative test scores often hide the sizeable proportions of their students who aren't receiving an education that prepares them for college, careers, or the work of citizenship. Such cases confirm a startling but still-hidden trend: the dearth of actual teaching in our schools.

The "Biggest Trend" in Education

ASCD author Barry Beers has kept records on visits to more than 5,000 classrooms. According to his data, two indispensable elements of effective teaching—clear learning objectives and checks for understanding—occur in fewer than 5 percent of classrooms (personal communication, 2010). This all accords with what I've observed in countless schools around the United States.

It also jibes with the findings of author and instructional trainer Michael Sonbert (2019). In a commentary for *Education Week,* he asks us if we "want to know what the biggest trend in teaching today is." Here's his answer:

> I bet you'll never guess it. The biggest trend in teaching today—
> from someone who's in dozens of schools and hundreds of

classrooms and who observes thousands of lessons every year—is that *teachers aren't teaching.*

You read that correctly. I'm not suggesting that teachers aren't working hard, because they are. I'm not suggesting that kids are just sitting in classes doing nothing (although sometimes they are). What I'm saying is that in most classrooms I visit, when students are working, they're usually working in *workbooks, on computers, or in groups.* (Sonbert, 2019; my emphasis)

Similarly, Lisa Delpit (2012) found herself shocked to find how little teaching was actually occurring in a variety of schools. After years of visiting classrooms, Richard Elmore (2006) wrote that "one of the most striking patterns to emerge is that teachers spend . . . relatively little time actually teaching" (p. 1).

Now there's a brutal fact—and an unparalleled opportunity.

As we'll see in Chapters 6 and 7, neither preservice nor school-based professional development equips teachers to provide high-quality, structured instruction. The problem is exacerbated by the absence of a coherent curriculum and a dearth of opportunities for teachers to develop and refine lessons with colleagues in true professional learning communities. To fill this void, a purported solution has emerged: online lesson banks (e.g., Teachers Pay Teachers [www .teacherspayteachers.com]). However, professional culture matters. The lessons are typically submitted and curated by educators who don't adequately understand the basic elements of effective teaching. Many sites consist of clever but unfocused activities, most of which are of poor quality.

According to a review of such sources by Morgan Polikoff and Jennifer Dean (2019), the sites are "bewildering and beg for curation." The lessons aren't aligned with the standards they ostensibly address; their reading, writing, and discussion tasks are weak and ineffectual. According to the researchers, most run from mediocre to not worth using. They don't solve the problem of subpar instruction; they perpetuate it.

A multitude of common but misconceived practices and products supplant or masquerade as authentic teaching, but I have found that the two most prominent examples are those that Sonbert (2019) notes: (1) the proliferation of low-quality worksheets and (2) excessive, unproductive group work. They're often simultaneous, a fact captured in the term *groupsheets*.

Substitute Teaching: Worksheets and Group Work

Walk through almost any school in the United States, and you'll discover that worksheets are *everywhere*. They have filled the breach left by the absence of curriculum and effective teaching. In hundreds of audience surveys, I've asked educators if they agree with me that worksheets are perhaps the lowest form of instructional material. There is immediate, audible agreement. Then I ask them to turn to their partners and estimate the percentage of the school day that students spend filling out worksheets. Their guesses average well above 50 percent, with a lot of them guessing between 60 and 80 percent. Then I tell them that their estimates match my perceptions and that classroom studies have confirmed those estimates for decades (Good & Brophy, 1997). Students spend about 6 of their 12 years in school completing worksheets.

Six years. That's a massive fund of precious time waiting to be repurposed toward reading, discussing, and writing as students acquire (by today's standards) enormous, intellectually enriching quantities of content knowledge. Those six years would enable us to shrink, if not shatter, the infamous opportunity gap. Repurposing classroom time in this way would ensure that the preponderance of our children would be ready for college, postsecondary training, or careers. It could mightily promote informed, contributive citizenship.

At their current level of use, worksheets kill these possibilities. They typically require students to engage in lower-order thinking— to fill in blanks, complete multiple-choice items, or provide short, regurgative answers to lower-order questions. They seldom demand extended thinking, explanation, or argument. They are designed to be completed in the absence of teaching; the directions found on most of them only short-circuit real instruction. They go a long way toward explaining a finding by Mehta and Fine (2019)—that *boring* is the most common word high school students use to describe school. Moreover, these ubiquitous, untested commercial products encourage a perverse routine in U.S. classrooms.

The Worksheet Scenario

After receiving limited instruction or directions, students are given their worksheet (often slowly, inefficiently). The teacher often sets no time limit for its completion. Because of this, about halfway through the period, the most conscientious students have usually completed the worksheet. The less diligent majority have barely started or might be halfway finished. This is either because they are dawdling or haven't been given adequate instruction—or both. They know the teacher typically won't collect the worksheets until the slowest students decide to finish.

Finally, the teacher collects the worksheets but seldom uses them to determine if or how well individual students or the class as a whole has succeeded on the assignment. Such routines squander hundreds of hours of class time every year without raising any eyebrows. Worksheets, sometimes dubbed *busy sheets* or *shut-up sheets*, often occupy the bulk of the period while making the teacher's job—in the absence of the curriculum they deserve—more manageable. Neither educators nor the public have acknowledged this catastrophe.

Education commentator Jennifer Gonzalez (2018) has noted the dominance of low-quality worksheets, not only in her numerous school tours but also in her own children's daily assignments. The worksheets have no connection to any conceivable curriculum, and according to Gonzalez, they abound in labeling and matching exercises, word scrambles, and *coloring*—right up through high school.

Although worksheets can pacify students, we underestimate how they bore and frustrate them. In a viral video, a frustrated high school student implores his teacher to "just teach us" instead of dumping "frickin' packets" of worksheets on them; then he walks out of class. (You can view the video on Gonzalez's blog at www.cultofpedagogy .com/busysheets.) Most students, though, inured to these routines, simply endure these substitutes for actual instruction, made somewhat palatable by another common feature of U.S. schooling: excessive group work. Because those worksheets are typically completed in groups.

Group Work: Disguised Inactivity?

No sensible educator rejects the efficacy of the proper amount of group work. And students need frequent, purposeful, usually brief opportunities to interact and articulate what they're learning during lessons. Group work, however, now occupies too much of the school day.

In words that may sound alien to today's educators, E. D. Hirsch laments the moment when desks were no longer arranged in rows, facing the front of the class. Why? Because it meant "the kids were no longer facing the teacher." This led to a precipitous decline in whole-class, frontal instruction. With exceeding frequency, students are now organized "into small groups and instructed to complete worksheets" (Hirsch, as cited in Riley, 2020a, para. 6).

This was a major, underappreciated development in schooling. It was buttressed by legitimate but overhyped research on cooperative learning. Group work caught fire, despite the caveats issued by our best researchers.

Robert Marzano is an advocate of cooperative learning, but he also issues a stern warning—that group work is frequently overused at the expense of more productive, whole-class methods (Marzano, Pickering, & Pollock, 2001). David Berliner and Ursula Casanova (1996) made the important discovery that the most productive form of cooperative learning isn't group work at all; it's having students work in purposeful pairs at certain junctures in the lesson. This arrangement increases accountability, engagement, and productivity, and it doesn't require students to turn their desks away from the instructor.

As Thomas Good and Jere Brophy (1997) point out, learning and attentiveness typically decline during group work, especially for the most vulnerable students. For these reasons, they warn practitioners not to employ it excessively.

I've found that educators are wholly unfamiliar with these cautionary findings on excessive group work. As a result, it has increased apace, driven by a zeal that prevents students from completing assignments on their own after receiving effective instruction. "Gone are the days of desk rows" enthuses the head of a major education organization. Gone indeed; group work now occupies about 70 percent of the school day (DeWitt, 2016).

But at what cost?

Collaborative Learning: The "Smog of Collaborative Effort"

Years ago, as a teacher in a middle school, I sat through multiple sessions on cooperative learning along with the rest of the faculty. We were given no guidelines or cautions on how often to apply it or for what spans of time. We were smitten and began to employ it liberally in our school.

It had no academic effect.

Tom Bennet is the head of researchEd, an organization whose goal is to dissuade educators from defaulting to practices that are popular but unsupported by evidence. As a teacher, Bennet (2015) used group work judiciously, noticing how others used it excessively—to students' detriment. He saw that beyond occasional or strategic use and employed within strict time limits, "group work easily devolves into disguised inactivity . . . as students put their backs into doing nothing, all hidden inside the smog of collaborative effort" (p. 8). Another researcher echoes these findings, lamenting the "social loafing" that too much group work encourages (Killian, 2017).

There's another unacknowledged problem here. Don't teachers notice, as Hirsch did, that in most classrooms, they're often looking at the side or back of students' heads? Don't we want students to be attentive to our words, gestures, and board work? Don't we want their work area to be in front of them—not off to the side? When I do demonstration lessons at schools, I request beforehand that I would like, if possible, for the desks to be in rows or at least facing forward.

Some educators gasp when I tell them that in high-performing countries like Finland, the default (though hardly exclusive) arrangement is desks arranged in rows (Stoltzfus, 2017). Teaching experts like Doug Lemov (2015) concur. He considers rows of desks facing forward as the ideal arrangement for most, but not all, learning.

Education Week's Alyson Klein (2020) recently reported about the mania for group seating at the expense of putting desks in rows. These arrangements, she writes, haven't promoted higher achievement but have often led to classroom management disasters—and to a dependence on worksheets ("groupsheets").

The Problem with Groupsheets

When group work becomes the dominant instructional mode, it often replaces, even precludes, full-length, whole-class structured lessons. These are impossible to provide for each individual group. Therefore, while the teacher is working with one student or group, the others need something to occupy their time. Worksheets are often the default solution.

The weaknesses of worksheets increase when we put students in groups to complete them. As anyone will observe, some students do the work, and others free ride. Alternatively, they divide the work randomly, giving the teacher no way to know who learned what.

My daughter routinely sat in such groups throughout her school years. She and her peers were often given multipage sets of worksheets with up to five days to complete their "frickin' packets." They lazily completed about a page a day, with some students dictating the phrase or sentence needed for the rest of the group to fill in the blanks with the pertinent facts or details. This often obviated the need to complete reading assignments or novels since everyone got full credit.

The unwholesome symbiosis of worksheets and (excessive) group work constitutes one of the most unfortunate, well-concealed features of schooling. In many schools, it constitutes the bulk of the real, "taught" curriculum. Its routines are so entrenched that we don't see how decisively they contribute to the "biggest trend" in education—the relative lack of actual teaching in our schools. All this hides from educators and the public, even as it perpetuates mediocrity and failure.

No researcher or education professor would deny or defend these facts about what happens in most schools. Nor would they deny their destructive effect. As I'll advocate in Chapter 8, professors of education could provide a vital service by condemning such routines. Indeed, the larger education community is dismayingly silent on them. You'll probably never hear a serious discussion of how to eliminate these patterns of malpractice at a faculty meeting, an administration meeting, or a board meeting.

Schools won't improve until we expose these routines and bring their effect to light—until we replace them with substantive training in effective instruction (more on authentic training in Chapters 6 and 7).

What would happen if we did? Here are some promising examples.

When Teachers *Teach*: The Effect of Structured Instruction

A 2nd grade team at Donaldson Elementary School in Tucson, Arizona, told me that only three or four of their 90-some students could write a decent descriptive setting for a story. Having taught them how to do this, the teachers assumed this skill was "developmental"—that is, too challenging for the grade level.

I then showed them how to employ a simple, efficient team protocol to design a structured lesson. It took about 15 minutes. It wasn't sexy, but it clarified what their previous lesson lacked—a series of steps culminating in students creating an interesting setting for their stories. Between each step, the teachers checked for understanding and quickly retaught when necessary.

As both Lemov (2015) and Goodwin (2011) point out, most effective lessons can appear pretty mundane. After implementing their lessons, these teachers told me that 88 of those 90 students could now write suitable (or better) descriptive settings. The experience opened their eyes to how explicit, structured instruction enables students to meet much higher expectations than educators presume across the curriculum.

This fact has enormous implications for our efforts to educate underperforming groups, close learning gaps, and address pandemic-era learning loss. It explains why surprisingly high proportions of students make substantial gains in a single year, even in classrooms with a wide range of previous achievement levels. It explains why 80 percent of my wife's algebra and geometry students passed the state math exam in a high school with a 90 percent poverty rate. Imagine how much higher that already high percentage would have been if students had received explicit, structured instruction in previous years.

In the previous chapter, I shared the story of English teacher Sean Connors, whose success with students led to his entire school achieving the largest gains on the state writing exam. Much of Connors's success was owing to his consistent use of explicit, structured instruction. He showed his students how to frame an argument, gather supporting evidence, organize it, then flesh it out in coherent sentences and paragraphs. On three occasions, I watched how Connors taught in small, manageable steps, each one accompanied by quick cycles of checking for understanding and reteaching. In this way, he was able to get almost every student to succeed on each phase of his lessons. He accomplished this in a highly diverse school with a poverty rate of more than 90 percent. About 98 percent of his students passed the state writing exam.

In Chapter 3, I described the dramatic single-year gains that two teachers I observed at La Cima Middle School achieved. Like Connors, they scaffolded every lesson on how to read analytically and write effectively—invaluable strategies in helping students acquire these skills. Their lessons were highly active—and interactive—with students frequently pairing up to assist one another and process each step in the learning. As a result of such teaching, their students' English language arts scores rose from the middle to the top tier in the state in one school year. I read the argumentative papers these kids wrote. I only wish the college freshmen I once taught had brought these middle schoolers' basic writing skills to my classes.

Several years ago, I came across a story about a dramatic turn-around at another school in Arizona: J. B. Sutton Elementary. Under the leadership of a new principal, it had risen from probationary status to above average, from a D to a B label in one school year. I requested a tour and wasn't surprised to find that the new principal and his lead teacher were adamant about structured instruction. Cold-calling, which keeps students attentive and engaged, was common throughout the school.

Author and consultant Harry Wong once remarked that the Flowing Wells School District in Tucson, Arizona, was the most impressive he'd studied (Schmoker, 2018). Under the leadership of former superintendent Robert Hendricks, the district provided extensive, ongoing training in structured instruction to every teacher, new or veteran. This resulted in an eight-year run of measurable improvement on state assessments.

In Massachusetts, Brockton High School's meteoric rise was a result of coherent curriculum infused with large amounts of "reading, writing, speaking, and reasoning," which became the school's mantra. Their success was also, according to then-principal Sue Szachowicz, a result of deep training in explicit instruction from education expert Jon Saphier.

The Los Angeles Unified School District studied its most effective teachers in the district's lowest-achieving schools (Poplin et al., 2011). The most effective teachers provided whole-class, teacher-directed "frontal" teaching. They "spelled out clear expectations for . . . what was to be learned," employed cold-calling, and "circulated throughout the lesson to check for understanding, keeping students on task" (pp. 40–41). They conducted whole-class discussions and used cooperative learning sparingly (but with frequent pair-sharing).

Moreover, these teachers did not differentiate expectations for their students. Instead, they scaffolded instruction and pushed their charges to succeed on grade-level work and materials. In discussions, they helped students communicate in clear, complete sentences.

Troy Prep High School in New York is the flagship school in Doug Lemov's Uncommon Schools network. Ninety-six percent of students live in poverty, and all teachers are trained in explicit teaching in their alternative preparation program. As a result, Troy students achieve at far higher levels than schools with the same demographics; in comparable schools, 40 percent of students passed the state math test in 2011. At Troy Prep, 100 percent of students passed. When the much more challenging Common Core math tests came along, the passing rate for high-poverty schools plummeted to 28 percent. Not so at Troy Prep, where 74 percent of students passed.

Now consider the effect that structured instruction could have in math nationally, where failure rates are highest. Dylan Wiliam (2007) conducted seminal work on the value of formative assessment, a virtual synonym for checking for understanding. If math teachers used formative assessment, he calculated, U.S. achievement in math would rise from 18th place to the top five on international rankings.

This brings us to the work of math curriculum expert John Mighton, who's convinced that the overwhelming majority of students could master high-level mathematics. As he told *The New York Times* (Bornstein, 2011), the reason kids don't is that few teachers actually scaffold. Only a few teach in small (I love this term) *micro steps*; even fewer check for understanding between steps and then reteach to address student misconceptions before moving on.

Mighton's math program—Junior Undiscovered Math Prodigies (JUMP)—does all these things, with the result that in some cases, "virtually every kid" learns, as their academic confidence climbs and their "math anxiety [is] diminished." A high-poverty school district near

London, England, used his methods with their lowest-achieving students. The percentage of students passing national tests rose from 12 to 60 percent—in one school year (Bornstein, 2011). We have to wonder how many more students would have passed had they received such instruction every year from every teacher.

At an elementary school in Vancouver, British Columbia, Mighton's program enabled every single student to achieve at the "fully meeting expectations" level in math. At a school in Ontario, teachers who received only two days of training in JUMP strategies were able to double the number of students passing standardized tests in math—five months after implementation (Bornstein, 2011).

Finally, a teacher at an independent school in Toronto was impressed with the results she achieved after she merely dabbled with Mighton's approach. She went all-in the following year and saw her students' class percentile average rise from 54 to 98 percent on the provincial math assessment. Further, the gap between high and low scorers narrowed dramatically (Bornstein, 2011). Such "whopping improvements" (Payne, 2007) are what we forfeit when we fail to implement structured teaching, where appropriate, in all classrooms.

The evidence for clear, coherent curriculum; for large amounts of purposeful reading, writing, and discussion; and for structured instruction can't be gainsaid. No school can fail to improve if its faculty focuses on these vital ingredients. Teachers would promote unprecedented levels of academic achievement, intellectual ability, prosperity, and—dare we hope?—civic and cultural maturity (Greenstone et al., 2012).

So why aren't schools implementing these powerful, straightforward elements? What root causes account for the calamitous gap between the best we know about educating our students and what actually happens in classrooms? This will be the subject of the next three chapters. These causes explain, as Elmore writes, why schools are always "aboil with change" that seldom leads to real improvement. They explain why there is "so much reform, so little change" in education (Payne, 2007).

How to Manage Instruction:
Action Questions for Leaders

- Do instructional coaches, providers of professional develop-ment, and professional learning community teams make every teacher's mastery of explicit, structured instruction one of their highest priorities?
- Does professional development, including faculty meetings, regularly feature the modeling of short but instructive seg-ments of effective teaching by instructional coaches, teachers, or administrators?
- Have leaders conducted an instructional audit to determine if students
  - Are employing the basic elements of structured instruction most of the time as a prerequisite to more independent learn-ing or projects?
  - Are not spending excessive time in groups doing work of ques-tionable value?
  - Are not completing low-level worksheets?
- Do teachers frequently cold-call students to ensure that all stu-dents are attentive?
- Have teachers been taught to cold-call in a way that prepares students to respond when called on (for example, by giving them opportunities beforehand to read, study, or prepare in response to questions or problems, sometimes after having a chance to discuss responses with a partner)? (Thank you, Stacie Zanzuc-chi, for making this clearer to me by calling this kind of question-ing *warm calling*.)

5

When Evidence Goes AWOL

Place a good person in a bad system,
and the system will win every time.

—Seymour Sarason

The preceding chapters made the case for the importance of curriculum, literacy, and instruction—the soul of schooling. We also looked at the many well-hidden but sobering facts surrounding our failure to make those elements our highest priority. In this chapter, we'll examine

- Representative pedagogic fads and distractions.
- Misconceptions and misperceptions about schooling that inform these fads and sustain the buffer.
- Runaway educational inflation and its effect on vital standards and expectations.

We'll see the damaging effects of a system whose priorities are driven not by evidence but by "whims, fads, opportunism, and ideology" (Corcoran et al., 2001, p. 80). The most unsettling features of that system hide behind a veneer of professionalism and are enabled by a culture of gullibility.

Pedagogic Fads and Distractions

In view of the evidence I've shared with you concerning the importance of curriculum, literacy, and effective instruction, you'd think there would be an all-out campaign to ensure their implementation in every U.S. classroom. Surely, there would be a massive national push, a groundswell of demand to make these elements our highest priority.

You'd be wrong. I recently scanned several weeks' worth of articles and education news. There wasn't a single citation, study, or case history urging us to adopt these priorities in light of the effect they would have on our students from the moment of implementation. Instead, I found pitches for such topics as integrating social media into instruction; increasing student engagement; purposeful play; personalized learning; innovative grading practices; "genetic analysis of students as a reform strategy" (seriously?); student-developed podcasts; place-based education; building your tech tool belt; and the case for "elemiddles."

Elemiddles? That article describes the move by numerous urban school districts to convert elementary and middle schools into K–8 schools (Field, 2021). As with many such articles, the author eventually admits that the research is mixed on whether it will have any effect on student outcomes, and there's no acknowledgment of the cost in time and disruption that such shifts incur. Every hour that districts invest in such low-priority initiatives robs their teachers of opportunities to build and implement a literacy-rich curriculum and receive training in highly effective teaching strategies.

Why go with something powerful and proven when you can opt for something "innovative" that doesn't require any meaningful change to existing instructional practice? Such distractions are the *weeds*, the competing species in the educational garden, the pseudo-reforms that divert our attention from our schools' most urgent, obvious problems.

Let's now examine some fads that co-opt mental and monetary resources we should be allotting instead to the highest-leverage strategies.

Grit and the Growth Mindset

As Christine Yeh (2017) writes in *Education Week*, the movement to promote grit in our classrooms became a national obsession. Its advocates aver that the key to success is sustained effort. This seems sensible enough. Educators became smitten with this notion, and with the idea that cultivating perseverance should be our primary focus—so they studied books, held conferences, and attended workshops. Millions of educators were encouraged to make grit a priority in their classrooms.

However, no one ever asked the pivotal questions: Do we know how to promote grit directly? Is there any evidence that training in this concept is more effective than, say, building and effectively delivering a coherent, intellectually engaging curriculum in schools that don't have one?

The answer to these questions is a resounding *no* (Willingham & Rotherham, 2020). Even its architects admit there's no proven way to promote grit in ways that have an effect on learning. "Forget grit," Yeh (2017) admonishes us; it's just another would-be panacea. We should focus instead on proven priorities that empower teachers and change students' lives.

The same goes for the "growth mindset," which advances the notion that a belief in effort (as opposed to a belief in innate intelligence) has an academic payoff. Its advocates would have us praise students for their hard work rather than for their intelligence (Sparks, 2021). Here, too, there's no reliable evidence that this focus has improved learning; there's no evidence it belongs on any list of what schools need most right now. Still, that didn't prevent it from becoming a household word in education circles and from being pursued as a solution to underachievement.

The effect of such initiatives isn't neutral. The investment in such pedagogic fads steals time and funding that educators could devote to learning to implement the highest-leverage evidence-based priorities.

If we want to cultivate grit or a growth mindset in students, we can best accomplish these things by focusing on curriculum, literacy, and effective instruction. Because they promote student success every hour and every day, they cultivate academic confidence, effort, persistence, and student satisfaction. They ensure significant increases in student outcomes. We know this; we have overwhelming proof from research and real schools.

The next family of popular innovations focuses on the promise of *individualization*. Effective teaching, the theory goes, must be customized for each child or group of children in accordance with their respective learning style, comfort level, culture, and interests. It hasn't worked. It continues to be what Bryan Goodwin (2021) dubs a "zombie idea," a wholly refuted, counterproductive concept that Just. Won't. Die.

Hyper-Individualization

The call for individualized education comes in several guises. The emergence of multiple intelligence theory, developed by Harvard University's Howard Gardner in the 1990s, gave it a huge boost. That theory advances the idea that we need to diagnose and categorize students by their intelligence (e.g., linguistic, artistic, mathematical, visual-spatial, bodily-kinesthetic). Almost immediately, educators and presenters began to propagate the idea that we needed to identify each student's dominant intelligence and then teach them in their respective mode. Gardner eventually disavowed such misunderstandings, although belatedly; the train had already left the station. It morphed readily into the idea that each child has a dominant learning style—a since thoroughly debunked concept (Goodwin, 2021; Willingham & Rotherham, 2020).

An article in *The Chronicle of Higher Education* is revealing. Erik Gilbert (2019), a history professor, heard a colleague from the education school refer to the importance of designing a course around students' individual learning styles. Gilbert was incredulous that a professor could be so ill informed. With a little digging, he discovered that the theory was alive and well; the education majors in his classes had been steeped in learning style theory. He later found out that more than 90 percent of teachers still embrace it, despite its being a classic neuromyth.

To this day, I meet teachers who believe they can and should diagnose and label students as spatial, artistic, or kinesthetic learners. Some take this a step further and insist that it's wrong to require students to learn or express their learning linguistically (in writing) or mathematically (in an equation). Nothing in our largely unmanaged, fad-driven system inhibits such erroneous thought. It informed the thinking of several of my daughters' teachers.

In an article in *Educational Leadership* (McKibben, 2020), one education scholar claims it is "pernicious" to require students to write equations in mathematical terms because it may be inconsistent with their learning style. They should be allowed, instead, to express their understanding artistically or dramatically. To not allow this, he suggests, is "profoundly discriminatory."

If some of these cases sound hard to believe, that's the point. They have bled seamlessly into a related movement, that of differentiated instruction. Differentiated instruction dictates that to educate a child, we must teach them individually or in small groups, with differing expectations and assignments because each student is unique in their needs and proclivities. Schoolwork should be based on an inventory of each child's personal interests, preferences, level of learning, culture—and (of course) learning style. This baseless notion has become so entrenched that it is built into virtually every teacher evaluation instrument. As we saw earlier, the French bought into differentiation and abandoned their highly effective, common content-rich curriculum to accommodate it. This resulted in an astonishingly steep decline at every level, with the largest impact on France's poorest students (Hirsch, 2016).

Differentiated instruction stands athwart the most firmly established principles of effective teaching. Fundamentally, it rejects the research that demonstrates that optimal benefits accrue to all students when teachers teach them the same lesson (Kirschner, Sweller, & Clark, 2010; Rosenshine, 2012). John Hattie's (2009) review of voluminous studies demonstrates that "the highest effect was when the same treatment was provided for all students and not varying the instruction depending on learning preferences" (p. 197).

Further, differentiated teaching greatly underestimates the power of scaffolding—of structured, whole-class teaching—in enabling students of varying abilities to learn from the same whole-class lesson. It also ignores the evidence of our best teachers and schools, such as those I've described in previous chapters. Every one of those teachers succeeded with every kind of student while relying, overwhelmingly, on whole-class, structured lessons.

Of course, such teachers do assign work that gives students meaningful choices; students can form and express their individual opinions and interpretations of literature and history, and they can choose from various options what they will research and write about. Indeed, good teachers have always provided extra assistance to students who struggle—usually at the end of the lesson, during the independent practice portion.

Every study confirms the manifest superiority of this model over a differentiated approach. As Bryan Goodwin (2011) writes in a comprehensive review of the research, there is simply no empirical evidence that differentiated instruction is effective. It is, in fact, *in*effective and has an especially negative effect on low achievers (Good & Brophy, 1997). In addition, differentiation all but necessitates a dependence on worksheets. Because overwhelmed teachers must customize lessons for numerous students or groups, they often default to the most accessible, if inferior, materials. As Hirsch (2016) observed, our experiment with hyper-individualization has turned schools into worksheet-driven, "soulless test-prep factories" (pp. 7–8).

This brings us to a related innovation, which also fails because it underestimates the power of effective whole-class instruction.

Response to Intervention (RTI)

Response to Intervention (RTI) spread across the educational landscape "like the latest diet fad" (Vanderheyden et al., 2016). Essentially, the instructional approach provides extra or individualized attention to students who don't learn from the initial daily lesson, known as Tier 1 in RTI parlance.

I've closely observed RTI programs in action. What everyone overlooks is the crucial fact that initial or Tier 1 instruction fails with struggling students because it typically lacks the elements of effective teaching. This leaves large numbers of students—sometimes the majority—needing extra help. I've seen how the need to provide extra or individual assistance to so many students often skews the school day. Schools often have to significantly reduce class periods to make time for the inefficient sorting, transitioning, and tutoring of so many students.

Is it effective? Not so much. According to an *Education Week* report (Sparks, 2011), it's "more popular than proven." RTI's use, writes the author, "is far outstripping its research base" (para. 1). Not only is it ineffective, it also has been shown to reduce levels of achievement among the low-achieving students it was intended to help (Sparks, 2015).

I've seen minimalist models of RTI work in schools where Tier 1 instruction was especially strong, but it typically fails to live up to expectations because it takes our eye off the instructional ball. It shifts attention from improving Tier 1 teaching (which guarantees dramatic gains in learning) to an overdependence on tutoring (Bryson et al., 2010). Moreover, the tutoring itself, the so-called Tier 2 intervention, often consists of low-quality, multiple-choice remediation exercises (Lipson & Wixson, 2008).

Here's the most interesting finding, though. When teachers provide effective, structured whole-class lessons, RTI is no longer necessary (Vanderheyden et al., 2016). A recent study of Algebra I courses vividly confirms this (Schwartz, 2021). It found that success in this gatekeeper course is best abetted by ongoing checks for understanding during the traditional class period. Remediation, on the other hand, is demotivating to many students and eats into class time, when all students should, instead, be learning rich, grade-level content—not completing remedial exercises. This holds all students back, but especially the ones being tutored, who are pushed further behind.

This is not to say that strategic tutoring isn't needed, especially as we recover from COVID-era learning loss. However, we need to offer it in an environment that ensures, first and foremost, high-quality Tier 1 instruction. Effective teaching increases student learning by a truly game-changing 35 to 50 percentile points—in just three years—and with no decrease in instructional time (Bracey, 2004; Marzano, 2007; Sanders & Horn, 1994).

RTI is a rich example of the perennial initiatives that become popular almost overnight and then become entrenched without anyone stopping to ask, "Are they effective?" Has anyone studied or road-tested the approach before springing it on unsuspecting schools and students?

The rush to embrace these approaches only postpones the realization that structured lessons are as effective as anything we know. As Hattie (2009) makes clear, we maximize our impact when we provide the same basic instruction to all students.

To illustrate, my wife taught algebra and geometry to 9th and 10th graders in a diverse, high-poverty school with large classes; some of those classes had as many as 40 students whose math backgrounds were all over the map. She honored her students and their culture, but her instruction was the same for all; learning styles weren't even on her radar. She had learned how to employ the elements of briskly paced, structured instruction as she taught the school's common math curriculum (which teachers created themselves in just two afternoons). She made daily learning targets crystal clear and assiduously checked for understanding on each small step of the lesson.

If students were confused, she didn't frantically attempt to tutor each one; she quickly retaught or broke the step down into more manageable micro-steps for the entire class, sometimes with students briefly assisting each other in pairs. At the end of her lessons, during the independent practice portion, she worked with the few remaining students who needed extra assistance. She learned all this on her own from reading books because training on structured instruction was never provided in her undergraduate preparation, her graduate coursework, or the professional development she received in three different school districts. As a result, more than 80 percent of her students passed a tough state math exam, significantly contributing to her school's dramatic, award-winning gains. According to differentiation theory, this should not have happened, certainly not in a diverse, high-poverty high school.

Such rich opportunities continue to elude us, with lamentable consequences for kids. Our failure to capitalize on the most efficacious practices ensures that a heartbreaking proportion will perform poorly in every subject area and that struggling students, who could be making great strides every year, will never catch up.

Let's now look at the most recent iteration of this trend: so-called personalized learning and its connection to educational technology.

Technology-Based Personalization

The late Robert Slavin noted that "technology may be fun, and it may be individualized, but it usually separates students from the personal attention of caring adults" (Marshall, 2021, p. 2). Technology and individualization are natural partners in the trend toward computer-based personalized learning. For many, this is the silver bullet that will save education. In this New Age, the computer becomes the primary instructor. Thus will we enter the promised land.

Does personalized learning stand up to the evidence? An entire issue of *Educational Leadership*—"Getting Personalization Right" (March 2017)—focuses on this question. Almost every article exudes optimism, but what you won't find is evidence of effectiveness. The issue's most honest article offers a searing critique (Riley, 2017). Benjamin Riley is the founding head of Deans for Impact, a group of courageous university-based education administrators who urge their members to stop purveying popular myths about learning. Instead, they exhort education departments to champion and train teachers in the most well-substantiated principles of instruction—those that have a significant effect on student outcomes. Riley pleads with his colleagues as "scientific professionals" to hold off on personalized learning. As he demonstrates, it's at odds with the most basic principles of how people learn. At best, writes John Pane of the Rand Corporation, "The evidence base [for personalized learning] is very weak at this point" (Herold, 2019, para. 30).

Personalized learning is only the most recent incarnation of our obsession with technology. I'm not saying we should discard computers or stop using them. I am saying, however, that we should heed the legion of eminent dissenters. They urge us to resist the utopian notion that technology-based approaches are superior to instructional practices we have yet to even train our teachers to implement.

As Doug Lemov writes,

> Low tech, high text. Read and read and read. Write and write and write. . . . The proliferation of technology affects students both directly—by degrading their attentional skills, for example—and indirectly—by crowding books out of students' lives. (Hess, 2022)

Michael Fullan (2010) also makes it clear that educational technology has never been a driver of school improvement. Decades of research confirm it has yet to have a significant effect on student learning, yet it still occupies a place of priority in what gets funded and implemented in schools.

"The problem," writes curricular expert Natalie Wexler (2020a), "isn't lack of access to technology, it's overexposure." Digital devices distract the most vulnerable learners and don't favor curriculum coherence; on the contrary, they "often serve to intensify the fragmented, decontextualized nature of American education." Moreover, computers "can't motivate [students] like a teacher can," and they can reduce already-scarce opportunities for productive discussion. For the late Steve Jobs, long experience taught him that no amount of technology would make a dent in schools until we tackle fundamental problems with what and how we teach (Carmody, 2012).

Bold predictions have been made for technology initiatives since the 1970s, yet as Slavin (2019) points out, their impact has been negligible: "Technology is still not ready for prime time, at least as far as teaching math and reading are concerned" (para. 9). The fact is, nothing surpasses the power of effective teachers who are armed with the right training and tools in schools where there is genuine instructional management.

When will we acknowledge this? Writers and researchers have studied the highest-performing school systems around the world. They discovered that technology played no role whatsoever in their success or improvement (Goodwin, 2011; Ripley, 2013; Stoltzfus, 2017). Bill Joy, cofounder of Sun Microsystems, expressed his dismay at the U.S. infatuation with educational technology in an interview with writer Mark Bauerlein (2009). He groused that high-achieving countries must take comfort in knowing that U.S. schools "are spending their time on this kind of crap" (p. 109).

I'm a fan of the right use of computers for writing and word processing, combined, in right measure, with pen-to-paper writing and note-taking, which have certain advantages over computers for promoting thinking and recall. Even so, every educator should reflect on the findings of a recent study of member countries of the Organisation for Economic Co-operation and Development (OECD) (Wexler, 2020a.) It revealed that "heavy computer use at a school had a negative impact on achievement" and that "vulnerable students are the most likely to be harmed by it." Instead of closing learning gaps, it "exacerbates existing inequalities." In short, the more hours students spend on computers, the lower their reading proficiency. That's because computer programs—like worksheets—are weighted toward atomized, lower-order skills and strategies that contribute minimally to students' ability to read critically, write, and articulate their thoughts.

Classroom Technology: When It Hits the Fan

I once toured the lowest-performing school in a district that aggressively advertised its excellence and emphasis on college preparation. The school had just received a large grant for a one-to-one initiative in which each student received a computer.

What did the principal and I see in our classroom observations? We saw personalized chaos: students working languidly and intermittently on various assignments, others working randomly, some drowsily and aimlessly exploring the computer's features. A few students were making stick figures for no apparent reason. We saw no reading or writing—and no teaching—in any of the classrooms. The principal, however, was ebullient. The new computers were getting lots of use.

A district in my home state of Arizona decided to abandon traditional frontal instruction and went all-in on the technology-centric classroom—to the tune of $33 million. The investment was so jaw-dropping and the effect so disappointing that *The New York Times* (Richtel, 2011) wrote an exposé on the project. Students worked in groups on various activities: blogging, listening to Kanye West, and building Facebook pages—to study Shakespeare. "Hope and enthusiasm are soaring here," wrote the *Times*, "but not test scores" (para. 6). If stories such as these seem extreme, think again. Such tech-based frivolities are now being officially encouraged as a replacement for reading and writing—by the National Council of Teachers of English (Schmoker, 2022).

I was later contracted to work on school improvement in one of the largest U.S. school systems. Every spare moment of teachers' time had been dominated by their one-to-one initiative. Years into the billion-dollar project, it was deemed a disaster, with no effect on student outcomes. The problem was fundamental; the district had never developed the most basic but still-overlooked element of high-quality education: a well-planned curriculum (Newcombe, 2015).

Has education technology evolved? Is it more effective now? In 2021, Bart Epstein (Tate, 2021), a long-time advocate of technology in classrooms, estimated that the United States spends as much as $75 billion each year on classroom technology. He believes it's time to shine "a substantial amount of sunlight on this industry" because "we don't know what works where, why, and under what circumstances.... Too many schools are buying things [tech tools] on a hope and a prayer and finding out later that . . . they didn't get their money's worth." Epstein adds, "There is no reason to believe any of this will change soon" (paras. 12, 19–20).

Misconceptions and Misperceptions

We've been looking at some popular but unproven pedagogic theories and initiatives—grit; hyper-individualized approaches, such as Response to Intervention; and education technology. We pursue them even as they postpone the implementation of the most effective teaching practices.

Our task, then, is to expose these illusory solutions and juxtapose them with their opposites—with the evidence-based actions that will truly transform schools. First, though, we must unmask certain widely accepted ideas that feed these insidious misperceptions—namely, that efforts at the school level are largely futile or can only improve learning at the margins. We must disrupt this perception; it prevents us from apprehending that swift, significant improvement is well within reach. These specious conceptions suppress reasonable, achievable expectations that parents and communities should have for their schools. They extinguish the hope and optimism that are essential to sustained effort by practitioners.

In the following sections, we'll examine some key misconceptions that promote misperceptions about what schools can achieve. As Elmore (1999–2000) makes clear, they are often fostered by the ingrained customs, messages, and internal workings of the administrative "superstructure of schooling."

Let's start with two widely accepted beliefs that inhibit constructive action to improve schools:

1. Schools can't improve until funding levels increase.
2. Effective schooling can only marginally ameliorate the effects of family income or poverty.

School Performance and School Funding

I once spent extended time with a new superintendent and an assistant superintendent of a district with several underperforming schools. During our time together, the superintendent would heatedly declare that no improvement could be expected until per pupil funding levels were increased. That week, we toured classrooms in several schools. Not one appeared to be implementing any common curriculum or providing effective instruction. This wasn't the new superintendent's fault; her predecessor had left the district in bad shape. None of the district's generous annual Title II allotment had been invested in desperately needed curricular and instructional priorities.

In the wake of these tours, nothing changed. The district failed to make any serious improvement efforts because the new district leadership suffered from the common misconception that their problem was a lack of funding. They regularly communicated this to school employees and the public.

In 2006, the Brookings Institute, a centrist think tank, launched the Hamilton Project to trace the relationship between educational attainment and school finances. It found that increases in per pupil spending have a limited effect on educational outcomes. Additional funding can enhance certain kinds of student programs and opportunities, and there is an argument that higher professional pay could attract and retain talented teachers (Will, 2019). I would love, for instance, to see additional funding invested in a four-period teaching day.

The real problem is that even large increases in school funding are almost never invested in the high-leverage actions most apt to improve student performance. As researcher Allen Odden (2009) informs us, "The problem isn't funding" (p. 22). It's primarily our failure to implement the best existing knowledge about how to educate students.

Not to mention that schools already receive dedicated funding to improve school quality. Additional money—beyond these existing amounts—played no role whatsoever in any of the successful schools described in the previous chapters.

You might remember the stunning success of New Dorp High School in the Bronx. As Peg Tyre (2012) takes pains to point out, no additional money was required to achieve the dramatic improvements that turned that school into an educational Mecca. The school simply used its existing allotments to train teachers in highly effective teaching strategies. All schools, in every state and district, receive such funds.

Adlai Stevenson High School, also in the Bronx, increased achievement levels for 10 years running. They achieved an 800 percent increase in students succeeding on advanced placement tests. As the late superintendent and author Rick DuFour would tell his audiences, these improvements at Stevenson didn't depend on additional funding; the high school reoriented its efforts and existing funds toward having teachers create high-quality curricula and then work in teams as professional learning communities to continually improve their instruction.

I offer a cautionary tale. Under the Obama Administration, certain low-performing schools received generous amounts of additional funding from the national School Improvement Grants (SIG) program. Seven years and $7 billion later—zilch. The grants had no impact on math or reading test scores, high school graduation, or college enrollment (Schaffhauser, 2017). According to *Education Week*, there was "no evidence that schools implementing SIG-funded models significantly changed student outcomes more or less than other similar low-performing schools" (Sparks, 2017, para. 3).

How can this be? Where does the money go?

We get an inkling from the postmortem report on the $200 million Zuckerberg initiative, which aimed to improve Newark, New Jersey, schools (Russakoff, 2015). The report, "Where the $200 Million Went," is revelatory. The money went toward subsidies for graduate school tuition, buyouts for unwanted staff, consultant contracts, administrative fees, the expansion of charter schools, data systems, strategic planning, teacher and principal reorganization of district office staff, the development of new evaluation frameworks, a teacher innovation fund, and so on. None of this had any effect on achievement. We underestimate the current system's capacity to spend profligately without ever addressing problems with curriculum, instruction, or supervision.

I once presented to the administration of an underperforming urban district that had received national press for spending over a billion dollars on new initiatives—with no impact on educational outcomes. Over lunch, I asked district administrators what they had learned from this experience. They talked enthusiastically about the various programs the new funding had made possible but seemed undisturbed that these had no effect on student achievement.

Let's now look at a related misconception—that family poverty prevents substantive school improvement.

Is Poverty Destiny?

Diane Ravitch, whose work I admire, once declared that poverty, not school quality, explained low achievement. However, as she acknowledges elsewhere (Tierney, 2013), schools do indeed improve when we replace "mindless test prepping" with what schools currently lack: "a rich curriculum in the arts and sciences, available in every school, for every child" (para. 18). That's a school quality problem—and a ripe opportunity. If we address that, then every child, rich or poor, will reap lifelong benefits.

Poverty's purported effect on learning deserves close consideration. To be sure, in classrooms that don't employ best practices, family income strongly corresponds to low achievement, and such factors as parents' education level are determinative. However, the impact of poverty is significantly reduced in schools and classrooms where best practices flourish. Poverty's effect on education can be likened to its effect on health and lifespan; in the absence of proper healthcare, poverty grimly corresponds to poor outcomes. Introducing high-quality healthcare has an enormous leveling effect; it drastically reduces differences in physical health among groups. As we've seen in previous chapters, some schools with the highest poverty rates attain outcomes similar to those with far more advantaged populations. Improved curriculum and instruction have enabled their students to overcome many of the effects of poverty and make swift, enormous gains on local and state assessments.

But these facts *aren't widely known*. So we plod on, oblivious to those methods that could have a decisive effect on children from

poverty. We also assuage our unease by attributing mediocrity or failure to factors beyond the school's control. These assumptions crush
hope and inhibit constructive action. They provide cover for the manifest shortcomings of schooling.

As Elmore (1999–2000) makes clear, "The buffer thrives on such
misconceptions and thus allows us to assign causality [for poor student
performance] to whatever our favorite theory suggests: weak family
structure, poverty, or discrimination" (p. 9). We should assign more of
that causality to our perennial failure to ensure high-quality curriculum and instruction in the great majority of schools. Every educator
should contemplate the words of Lisa Delpit (2012), who writes,

> It is easy to choose poverty as the reason for poor performance. . . .
> Blaming poverty works out for school systems because then you don't
> have to change your lesson plans! "Blaming poverty" absolves the
> school of its duty to reckon with its shortcomings. It wrongly shifts
> responsibility to factors it can't control. (p. 7)

Many trusted sources speak to the fact that good schooling can
appreciably overcome the effects of poverty:

- Rick DuFour and Robert Marzano (2011) cite the work of Kati
  Haycock, whose work demonstrates that "in the hands of our
  most effective teachers, the effects of poverty and institutional
  racism melt away" (p. 65).
- Linda Darling-Hammond (2010–2011) points out that sound
  curriculum alone can erase the daunting gaps among entering
  kindergartners.
- According to E. D. Hirsch (2016), ensuring that students acquire
  a command of standard English would all but eliminate most of
  the gaps among socioeconomic groups.
- In high-poverty Pueblo, Colorado, a focus on literacy and on the
  abandonment of the Crayola curriculum resulted in tremendous
  gains—from 12 to 64 percent in reading and 2 to 48 percent in
  writing over two years (Schmoker, 1999).

- Mike Rose (1989) grew up so poor that he shared a bedroom with his parents in their tiny home. In 10th grade, his English teacher had students read and discuss vastly more books and articles— and reflect on them in writing—than any of Rose's former teachers had ever done. It put Rose on a path to becoming a professor at the University of California at Los Angeles and a noted author.

Alas, the misconceptions that funding and poverty are determinative are often advanced by the larger educational system—by the "superstructure of schooling." It creates the pretense that schools already operate on logical, proven practices, although most don't (Elmore, 1999–2000, p. 6).

This false confidence is increasingly cultivated through organized efforts by school districts themselves. On several fronts, it represents "the triumph of public relations" (Ravitch, 2011). Such efforts placate parents and the public while diverting attention away from aspects of schooling that cry out for reform.

Public Relations and Parental Misperceptions

As we've seen, Americans tend to give high marks to the schools their *own* children attend. These perceptions suppress all-important demands for better schooling. These positive perceptions are further encouraged by the public relations arm of modern school districts. Many have full-time, in-house public relations staff that employ a variety of effective tools: newsletters, billboards, electronic signage at schools, ads in movie theaters, and so on. All proclaim a commitment to academic excellence, and many bedeck school hallways with college pennants to convey an aura of serious academic work, despite the patent mismatch between K–12 practices and college requirements (Conley, 2007; Varlas, 2016).

Parent nights often contribute to this glossy image. In attending many over the years, I always noticed how the schools hit all the right notes. Like all parents, we wanted to believe our kids were receiving a high-quality education. Parent surveys reflect the success of these efforts. More than 75 percent of parents give their local school an *A* or *B* rating, and more than 90 percent believe their children are performing at grade level. In fact, less than one-third perform at grade level (Petrilli, 2017).

If we care about education, then we must ask, with Michael Petrilli (2018), if more honest, accurate reporting isn't the key. Schools must begin "shooting straight with parents about how their daughters and sons are performing" (para. 1). Would such honesty create, as Chester Finn and David Steiner (2019) ask, the kind of intensified pressure on schools that would make them better? That should be our hope.

Educational Inflation

The fact is, the superstructure of schooling imparts an unwarranted degree of trust in a system that betrays its promotional rhetoric. That trust is the result of another insidious feature of the buffer: educational inflation. It takes a variety of forms.

Rankings, Ratings, and Awards

If a school or district receives an impressive state or regional ranking or rating, it will tout this in local newspapers and in signage and murals on school building walls. People are often delighted to have their children attend award-winning schools even if—unknown to them—school quality is average or worse.

I once worked in a chaotically run underperforming district, but because we ranked above the less-advantaged school systems in the region, the district leadership took every opportunity to publicly proclaim that we were "number one." The tendency to inflate schools' accomplishments is especially pronounced in the distribution of state ratings. I've seen how *A* and *B* ratings are promiscuously distributed to schools that are mediocre or worse; *C*s are rare, and to earn a *D* or an *F*, a school has to perform deplorably.

I've observed and consulted in numerous schools that received the coveted *A+* rating only to discover that the honorific bears little relation to school quality. Soon after being hired at an *A+* school, I complimented my principal on our award. He shrugged and told me how it was the result of a lengthy application process, with assistance from the district's public relations director. I thought he was being humble—until I saw our school's mediocre test scores. I eventually discovered that instruction, especially in literacy, was exceptionally poor. That same year, I learned that the coveted Blue Ribbon school awards were often granted irrespective of exceptional achievement (Schmoker, 2006).

Socioeconomic advantage often contributes to high ratings, yet in touring every kind of school in multiple states, I have seen the same quality of instruction in affluent *A+* schools as I have seen in high-poverty schools with low ratings. I did extensive consulting at a school that had better-than-average test scores, but I was brought in precisely because the principal could see how the school was failing the majority of its students. Every classroom visit confirmed this. Nevertheless, there was no pressure from parents to improve performance at this highly rated institution.

I've become similarly disenchanted with individual awards for teachers and administrators. These also bestow prestige on their respective schools and districts. For many of them, it's all about paperwork, gimmickry, and campaigning. Some of the least effective teachers I've observed received Teacher of the Year awards—and I've seen very personable but instructionally disengaged administrators receive the highest state and national honors.

I always want to ask the award-granting agencies, "What did you see when you visited these schools?" Did they see, as I did at one such school, how students routinely colored and made posters in English and social studies? I doubt that parents had any idea such things were occurring in their *A+* school with its highly decorated administrator.

Ratings, rankings, and awards are features of a broader culture of inflation, which includes graduation rates, grades, academic standards—and teacher evaluations. Taken together, they degrade students' life prospects.

Lies, Damned Lies, and Graduation Rates

We need accurate information and data about schools to identify crucial needs and exploit opportunities for improvement. No statistics are less accurate than graduation rates. As Robert Pondiscio (in Wright, 2018) attests, they are "the phoniest statistics in education" (para. 11). Several years ago, President Barack Obama gave a commencement address to a high school audience, praising faculty and students for doubling their graduation rate. What he didn't share with the audience—and may not have known—was that *only 16 percent* of those graduates had met minimal state reading standards (Ravitch, 2011). At a high school in Denver, Colorado, the president praised students and faculty for their swift ascension to a 97 percent graduation rate, but only 10 percent of its students met state science standards. In math, they were performing in the bottom 5 percent, and in reading and writing, the bottom 1 percent (Ravitch, 2011).

Around that same time, Secretary of Education Arne Duncan praised a Chicago-area school for its stellar graduation rate, which had risen well above that of Chicago Public Schools. It was later discovered that only 17 percent of students at that school had actually passed their state tests. That's well *below* average for Chicago schools (Ravitch, 2011).

Likewise, consider these more recent numbers from Minneapolis Public Schools. In five years, the graduation rate rose from 49 to 64 percent. During that same period, the reading proficiency rate declined precipitously, from 57 to 32 percent (Foley, 2016).

That such mendacity could evade notice should disturb us deeply. It speaks to education's not-so-innocent capacity to hide its failings, and these are not isolated cases. The national adjusted cohort graduation rate for U.S. public high school students was a record-shattering 88 percent in 2021, even as NAEP scores stagnated or declined (Gewertz, 2018).

Grade Inflation in a Broken System

The key contributor to these grossly inflated rates is rampant grade inflation, which, according to *Education Week*, is a national problem.

It has become increasingly common for teachers to give good grades to students who haven't earned them or who rarely attend classes (Gewertz, 2017). This is deeply destructive of learning. As Madeline Will (2020) reports, students learn more when teachers are tough graders. Will found that regardless of student background, "no matter how you slice it, everybody benefits from high grading standards" (para. 14).

Literacy educator Juliet Wahleithner (2020) recently interviewed a number of first-generation college students who described the shock of their first year in college—how unprepared they were for the reading and writing demands of college coursework, even though they had received excellent grades in honors courses in their high schools. We can trace much of the stratospheric increase in high school graduation rates to programs where the criterion for passing is risibly diluted.

Take credit recovery, for instance, a program that is not well known to the wider public, despite being at the center of our current "graduation rate malfeasance" (Wright, 2018). In credit recovery, potential dropouts—those with abysmal grades and attendance—retake previously failed courses; these courses are (*ahem*) "accelerated" but watered-down versions of the courses they need to graduate. As *The New York Times* discovered, students can earn a full semester's credit by investing only 10 hours of work in a course (Gardner, 2015).

I've mentored students in credit recovery programs who were about to flunk out of high school. Two weeks later, I found out that one had passed her most difficult course with above-average grades. A nephew of mine received full course credit for English—by filling out a handful of worksheets and reading a single book written several years below his grade level. No writing was required.

New York City schools offered a credit recovery course called Project Graduation. One teacher was assigned to "teach" as many as 35 required subjects simultaneously. Almost all those subjects were outside her area of expertise. That didn't matter because students only had to fill out individual course packets to meet requirements (Gonzalez, 2015). Absenteeism was rampant, but graduation rates soared, from 61 to 74 percent in one school year.

Such oddities are a direct result of our failure to provide teachers with any semblance of legitimate curriculum. This leaves them to define *success* entirely on their own, with little or no guidance, however much it compromises even the most minimal standards.

The Silent Devolution of Standards

These trends comport with a larger decline: a collapse in academic standards (Tucker, 2015). This gradual but ultimately dramatic downward trend went undetected by the public and many in the K–12 community. We saw earlier how literacy standards have suffered, how assigned readings are now several grade levels lower than assigned texts in the recent past (Paulson, 2014; Stotsky, 1999), and how only 17 percent of assignments are on grade level. This is especially pronounced in schools with government-subsidized meals and students of color. This is despite the fact that such students perform much better when given more challenging, grade-level work (TNTP, 2018).

In the important area of writing, *there are no standards whatsoever.* The ability to write clear, coherent prose is no longer a requirement to pass courses or graduate from high school. Many students graduate without ever receiving meaningful instruction in writing (Darling-Hammond, 2010–2011; Dillon, 2004; Reid, in Harris et al., 2008).

Another troubling trend: Oregon recently joined dozens of other U.S. states that have abolished exit exams in the last decade. This is commensurate with rampant inflation in grades and graduation rates. Few, if any, objective standards now exist against which to gauge student learning. There's no way to know if schools are effectively imparting academic knowledge of math, civics, history, science, and reading and writing ability.

Our indifference to this downward drift in standards and expectations has culminated in a diploma with limited value. In Chicago Public Schools, only 26 percent of high school students are at grade level in reading and math (Kessler, 2021). Such achievement levels fuel high college dropout rates and truly alarming community college failures, which represent an enormous waste of time and money. Only

16 percent of urban community college students will graduate in three years or less (Samuels, 2022).

According to the Washington, DC–based Alliance for Excellent Education, high school students "are being allowed to walk across the stage at graduation with a 'paper-thin' diploma" (Gewertz, 2017, para. 4). An *Education Week* article, appropriately titled "Who Gets Hurt?" (Gewertz, 2017), finds that only about 30 percent of high school graduates are prepared to succeed in college or the workplace. This is inexcusable and has lifelong consequences for the students we claim to care about.

One barrier in particular inhibits efforts to improve instructional performance or recognize our failure to implement superior practices: inflated teacher evaluations.

Teacher Evaluation: The Mirage of Instructional Supervision

Instructionally focused principals have a pivotal effect on school effectiveness. They spark big gains in student learning because they can potentially multiply the benefits of effective instruction by the number of teachers they supervise (Superville, 2021). Indeed, thousands of books and conferences are devoted to instructional leadership. We've developed elaborate supervisory protocols that might convince us that school administrators are meaningfully evaluating curriculum and instruction to ensure quality and improvement.

We'd be wrong. These systems only create the illusion that schools take instructional supervision seriously. As Kim Marshall (2005) observes, one of education's greatest ironies is the prevalence of "ridiculously thin supervision of the school's most important employees"—its teachers (p. 728). Teaching may, in fact, be the least supervised profession. This allows malpractice to thrive even as virtually all teachers receive good or excellent ratings on annual evaluations.

As a new teacher, education researcher Tony Wagner (2004) knew he had plenty to learn. However, when he received his first evaluation, he was shocked to discover he "was proficient at everything, it seemed" (p. 40). That is how most of my own teacher evaluations went, before I had mastered even the most basic elements of good teaching.

As Chester Finn (2017) points out, we have obsessed over policy and school structure for decades, but we've failed to focus our efforts on "what really matters in the education of children, namely what and how they are taught" (para. 1). In our upside-down education system, managing "what and how students are taught" has become a sidebar for which few principals received meaningful training. In his presentations, Rick DuFour would compare pilots to principals. A pilot's highest priority is to fly the plane. A principal's highest priority should be to conscientiously supervise and ensure high-quality curriculum and instruction, but the job of the principal has evolved to a point where, as DuFour would chide us, most principals do everything except "fly the damned plane."

As Elmore (1999–2000) makes clear, administrators don't monitor or manage—that is, observe, advise, and hold employees accountable for—sound instruction. They're not trained for this. Few were proficient in instruction or were master teachers before they became administrators. As a result, "direct involvement in instruction is among the least frequent activities administrators perform." Most of them, Elmore found, are "untrained for leading instructional change. They are socialized to be maintainers" of the status quo (pp. 2–3).

It's worth repeating: Schools only improve when administrators frequently observe and constructively coach teachers toward effective practice. Right now, though, principals rarely visit classrooms except to conduct elaborate annual "evaluations."

The Madness of Teacher Evaluation Instruments

Do these formal exercises promote improvements in what and how students are taught? They do not. A study sponsored by the Gates Foundation found that teacher evaluation is largely pro forma (Stecher et al., 2018). Despite the alarming gap between effective and actual practice, almost no instructor is deemed "in need of improvement."

This side of criminal malfeasance, teachers are almost never terminated for poor performance. In the entire state of California, for instance, only 62 teachers out of 220,000 lost their jobs in a five-year period (Miller, 2003).

To address this problem, the Gates Foundation launched a multiyear, multibillion dollar initiative to reform teacher evaluation. This led to the development of several preposterously elaborate evaluation tools, all crammed with specious pedagogic criteria. Even the most defensible elements of these tools were rendered in unhelpful, ambiguous "educationese."

The architects of the tools tacitly admit they were overlong, confusing, and not useful for improvement purposes (Danielson, 2015; Goodwin, 2011). This project demonstrated, according to one expert, education's "unwavering commitment to unproven approaches" (Anderson, 2012, para. 7). The entire decade-long project constituted an "unforced error of enormous magnitude" (Petrilli, 2015, para. 5). In the end, it had zero impact (Will, 2021). This boondoggle demonstrates education's eagerness to project an image of competence to protect itself against outside "inspection, interference, or disruption" by parents, the public, or other entities (Elmore, 1999–2000, p. 6).

As we've seen, every study reveals a great majority of teachers are in desperate need of training in the most fundamental elements of instruction; only a small fraction now implement them (Elmore, 1999–2000; Odden & Kelly, 2002; Sonbert, 2019). Most principals are in on this secret. They officially designate only 2.7 percent of their teachers as "in need of improvement," but in surveys, they indicate that 28 percent are in such need—about 10 times as many (Kraft & Gilmour, 2017). Our failure here perpetuates mediocrity, with grave consequences for our lowest-achieving students.

The Effect of Misconceived Teacher Evaluation

I once met a social studies teacher who taught in one of the least advantaged schools in his metropolitan area. He bragged that he got great evaluations but spent most of his time chatting with his students about popular topics, such as his favorite rock groups. He told me no administrator had ever given him a poor evaluation, despite the gaping hole he left in his students' civic and historical knowledge.

I once consulted in a high-poverty elementary school. A personable 1st grade teacher there had received excellent evaluations for more than 20 years, but he barely taught. He had developed elaborate, time-killing rituals for taking attendance, followed by various group activities, followed by students singing a dozen or more songs—all during the reading block. His students performed miserably (although they did sing well). He had never received any feedback from his principal telling him to improve his instruction. He was popular in the community because everyone attributed low achievement at the school to . . . family poverty.

I referred earlier to some of my daughters' teachers—to a social studies teacher who routinely digressed for long periods and an English teacher who had no interest in teaching writing. When I confronted the principals in each case, I was told that none of the administrative training they received prepared them to monitor curricular content or instruction. Not one teacher was on any kind of improvement plan, and all of them had received the highest ratings on their annual evaluations. These teachers didn't need stellar evaluations; they needed targeted support and training.

Let's look, lastly, at two more elements of the K–12 superstructure: accreditation agencies and well-meant but unfortunate theories that would legitimize inflation by weakening standards and expectations.

Accreditation Inflation

Every few years, schools in the United States must undergo an expensive, multifaceted study of their personnel, finances, curricula, and resources. This is accompanied by on-site observations by a team of officials from a regionally sanctioned accreditation agency. The agency's job is to certify that the school conforms to adequate standards of quality and performance.

Most schools get their seal of approval. Schools with no meaningful curriculum pass muster, as do those with no routines for monitoring or improving instruction. Schools that rely heavily on worksheets, movies, and excessive group work pass with flying colors. Mostly all get certified.

The final accreditation reports tell us little about school quality. When I interviewed two high-ranking officials from a multistate accreditation group, they admitted to knowing almost nothing about the ground-level quality of curriculum and instruction at the schools they certify.

These various forms of inflation have evolved over decades, undetected because they developed gradually and largely out of sight. They quietly corrode learning standards even as they conceal the inferior quality of most schooling—as well as its consequences. This erosion of student expectations has a particularly unfortunate effect on underprivileged students whose abilities we underestimate. For Lisa Delpit (2012), low expectations reflect historic, misbegotten "beliefs about Black children and learning." We must, she insists, "recognize the brilliance of poor, urban children and teach them *more* content, not less" (p. xix).

That is becoming more difficult.

Normalizing Underachievement

If all this were not enough, new emergent theories will likely reduce academic and career expectations for poor and marginalized students (Bergner, 2021). Some would diminish the importance of learning gaps or deny their existence altogether (Pondiscio, 2021c). Several eminent education leaders, working from these ideas, now deny the existence of COVID-19-era learning loss (*Los Angeles Times*, 2021). Still others seek to abolish grade-level expectations and the idea that any student is ever behind in their learning (McKibben, 2020). Some of the most prominent postulators denigrate academic knowledge itself; they would rather redefine *achievement* around virtually unmeasurable nonacademic criteria (Bergner, 2021; Hess & Addison, 2020).

If acted on, such ideas would leave students less prepared than ever for college, careers, and the duties of citizenship (Bergner, 2021; McWhorter, 2021; Pondiscio, 2021c). They would exacerbate a problem that plagues millions of students.

Take the case of Precious, for instance (La Salle & Johnson, 2019). When she struggled in 1st grade, the school didn't examine the quality of instruction she was receiving; it simply placed students like her in special education classes, where learning expectations were severely reduced. She met all those expectations through 4th grade, but she was only being given 1st grade work.

Then an enlightened administrator arrived at the school. He knew that learning gaps and learning loss were real. He knew it was irresponsible to regard 1st grade work as 4th grade achievement and that this would cripple students such as Precious. Consequently, he raised expectations schoolwide—and students began to meet them. By the end of 5th grade, both Precious and her sister had made tremendous progress and were eventually able to exit special education.

As the editorial board of the *Los Angeles Times* (2021) put it, "Learning loss is real," and we should "stop pretending otherwise." Instructional experts Paul Bambrick-Santoyo and Stephen Chiger (2021) concur: "What equity does *not* mean is lowering the bar to where students happen to be currently. Embracing equity means building challenging curriculum . . . because it is good for kids" (para. 13).

We should always be examining what we assess students on and how we assess them; this is healthy. I would advocate for more curriculum-based high school exit exams, with a more generous writing component. We should not, however, capitulate to a radical call to abandon grade-level expectations or assessments of academic knowledge, intellectual skills, and literacy. This will only amplify the problem. The effect of lowered expectations on students of color is well established (Delpit, 2012) and is a national shame.

Finally, in any discussion of high expectations, we should remember that vastly more kids will meet them when we implement the most effective evidence-based practices and make school more intellectually engaging.

The Price of Misperception—And Malpractice

Add it up—the public relations, the inflated grades, the graduation rates and school awards, the proliferation of educational fads and misconceptions, and the insidious decline in standards and expectations. These are all elements of the buffer. Together, they conceal or blur the distinctions between poor and effective schooling; they prevent us from perceiving the most crippling shortcomings of the current system.

What are the consequences of this failure to exploit our richest opportunities for better schools? Hidden below the water line, the ship of schooling has more than a few minor leaks; it has large gashes in its hull. That has serious consequences for those on board.

The Academic Consequences

Here are some of the academic consequences:

- About half of U.S. 3rd graders read below grade level (Wu, 2010). Eighty percent of these students remain poor readers into high school (Sparks, 2020a), and they are four times as likely to drop out of high school (Hernandez, 2012).
- In 27 large, urban U.S. school districts, 8th grade math proficiency rates run between 4 and 24 percent (McGurn, 2021).
- Fewer than 25 percent of high school graduates who enroll in two-year colleges complete a degree in three years (Hanson, 2022). For those who attend schools in urban areas, that number drops to 16 percent (Samuels, 2022).
- Only 14.7 percent of recent high school graduates complete a bachelor's degree within six years (Hanson, 2022).
- According to the Organisation for Economic Co-operation and Development (OECD), millennials in the U.S. workforce are tied for last place on tests of mathematics and problem solving (Tucker, 2021).
- According to *Library Journal* (Rea, 2020), we're in the midst of a true literacy crisis. Forty-three million Americans are in the "illiterate/functionally illiterate" category.

The Social Consequences

Here are some of the social, economic, and life consequences that follow from inferior schooling:

- About 70 percent of incarcerated individuals cannot read at a 4th grade level. "The people we lock up," writes David Kirkland (2019), "are the same people we fail to teach to read and write" (p. 10).
- An assessment of students at a prestigious university found that even the highest achieving students tend to "accept the word of experts at face value" (Graff, 2003, p. 68). In our media-drenched era, that's worrisome.
- About one-third of employees in blue-chip companies write so poorly that they need remedial instruction. This is a significant drain on organizational and employee productivity (Dillon, 2004).
- U.S. millennials, according to Marc Tucker (2021), may be the worst-educated workforce in the industrialized world.
- If the United States were able to close even half of its achievement gap with Canada, the economic impact would pay for Social Security's and Medicare's shortfall, an amount 10 times larger than the economic losses from the Great Recession of 2008 (Hanushek, 2018).

These findings translate to poor health outcomes, lower standards of living, and reduced lifelong earnings and wealth accumulation. They restrict our children's ability to find interesting, contributive occupations, and they affect our ability to fund college costs, infrastructure, and healthcare.

The Cultural Consequences

Should we, as a nation, be concerned about the growing extremism on both ends of the political spectrum, which holds the rest of us hostage? Citizens on the far left and right brandish loaded slogans. As

George Orwell taught us, these quash, not encourage, independent thought. The miseducated have no defense against such manipulative language.

How many of those who embrace extreme views would moderate them if they had grown up in school systems that furnished them with hundreds of hours and dozens of opportunities each year to

- Read multiple sides of historical and cultural issues?
- Examine pertinent data from a range of sources?
- Discuss multiple perspectives in a thoughtful, civil fashion, with an emphasis on listening carefully before responding?

Wouldn't such a school system produce a more judicious, fair-minded, civil populace—one more open to compromise and able to appreciate the best thinking found along the political spectrum?

If enough concerned educators and citizens develop a deep, energized awareness of such facts, I believe they will animate change and begin to move the needle. I'll suggest strategies for promoting more widespread awareness in Chapter 8. Once we achieve that awareness, the primary agents of that change could well be teacher preparation, professional development, or both. These are the subjects of the next two chapters.

How to Avoid Pedagogical Fads and Educational Inflation: Action Questions for Leaders

- Does your school or district
  - Select its priorities strictly based on what the evidence deems to be most essential to student success: curriculum, literacy, and effective instruction?
  - Monitor and maintain accurate grading practices and high expectations, matched with effective practice, to maximize student success?
- Do district communications and parent nights provide the community with honest, adequate information about what students

are learning? Can you guarantee that it squares with claims about college preparation (e.g., in terms of the amount and frequency of reading, discussion, writing, and writing instruction students will receive)?

- Does your professional development routinely present research and school evidence that reinforce the fact that high-quality curricula and effective instruction greatly mitigate the effects of poverty?

- Does teacher evaluation provide frequent, honest, and constructive feedback to practitioners to ensure not only their fidelity to the agreed-on curriculum but also their use of the most effective instructional methods?

6

The (Mis)Education
of Educators

Teacher education is the Dodge City of the education world.
Like the fabled Wild West town, it is unruly and chaotic.

—Arthur Levine

Years ago, I ran into a district colleague on the campus of the local university. At some point, I referred to some dramatically improved schools I'd visited or read about. He had never heard such stories. He'd been taught that achievement was a function of socioeconomic factors and that efforts to improve curriculum or instruction were largely futile. I asked him where he had learned this. He pointed to the education building behind us and said, "Right here. I'm just finishing up a doctorate in education."

Higher education, writes Marc Tucker (2018), "is the weakest link" in the K–12 system. For Robert Pondiscio (2014), it's the root cause of our underachieving schools. I have to agree. Education's theoretical, often antiscientific ethos has corrupted professional development, which is a shame: Teacher and administrative preparation programs could be the primary drivers of systemic, large-scale improvement if they would embrace the work of our best researchers. For that to happen, such preparation programs must first have an encounter with their own "brutal facts."

The Problem: The Education of an Educator

I have observed and been intermittently involved with university-based educational programs for several decades. I have a doctorate in education. In my coursework, I never learned the most critical information in the three areas I outlined in Chapters 2, 3, and 4: curriculum, literacy, and effective instruction. In only one course did I learn anything about schools that made significant gains—or how they made them. I learned this from an adjunct professor who was a working school administrator. (Thank you, Mary Beth McCorkle!) To become an effective educator, I had to unlearn much of what I learned in these institutions. Regarding instruction, I learned more in just a few hours from one mentor teacher than from the totality of my education classes.

I still remember a few details from the orientation for new education majors. A tall, handsome professor, beaming with confidence and glancing for approbation from his colleagues on the dais, declared that our school of education was among the best in the United States. I felt lucky to be there. My professors were kind, conscientious people who worked hard to provide the standard fare of such programs. I liked these people in whose classes I learned about the history of public schooling, various philosophies of education, educational psychology, and prominent scholars and educational theories.

However, if a well-prepared teaching force was the school's goal, it failed. I—and my classmates—left the program completely unprepared to teach. We learned about philosophical ideas, movements, and abstract theories of curriculum, but we were never taught how to impart literacy skills or teach an effective lesson.

My English Methods course was especially disappointing. It was taught by a charming woman regarded as a legend at the school. What did we learn from her? We learned how to create individual learning kits in pocket folders that contained worksheets, crossword puzzles, and literacy-themed board games. We were encouraged to have students make and illustrate elaborate book covers. We were assigned to make such things ourselves. Having had outstanding literature professors in college, I silently smoldered, noting that my grade would depend on developing such packets and on the bulletin board I had to design and present to the class. I was aghast—and surprised at the alacrity with which my classmates took to these activities.

At no time did we ever learn how to

- Develop compelling questions about literary works or avoid asking dull, lower-order questions.
- Conduct an effective discussion in which all students participated.
- Teach writing or grade a written assignment.
- Scaffold instruction on analytic reading or expository writing by breaking the work into manageable steps while circulating in the classroom to see where reteaching was in order.

What of the final phase of undergraduate teacher preparation—student teaching?

Student Teaching: Sink or Swim

I eagerly looked forward to student teaching, anxious to learn from the mentor teachers to whom I was assigned. Alas, their instruction reflected the same deficient preparation I had already received. In both cases, there was no curriculum to guide us in what content or skills to teach; my mentors made it up as they went along. Worksheets, filmstrips, and arts and crafts activities dominated their teaching. Little of it had any connection to literacy and almost none of it to college or career readiness.

After this disappointing experience, I approached the university officials who were responsible for my placement. They were refreshingly receptive and apologetic, admitting that there was no real screening process for selecting mentor teachers and no guidance or requirements for what they should teach us—none whatsoever. The only criteria for selecting them seemed to be their readiness to take on a student teacher. Not much changed in the decades between my undergraduate experience and my own involvement in teacher education.

Fast Forward: Different Year, Same Problems

Years later, I did a temporary stint in a teacher preparation program. The clinical professors met monthly. At my first meeting, we critiqued videos of the program's student teachers in action. The comments that ensued were surprisingly imprecise and upbeat. My colleagues seemed intent on simply checking off the dozens of criteria in the evaluation template with which the university had saddled them. The group didn't seem to discern fatal weaknesses in these lessons, which presumably represented their student teachers' best work.

I ventured to ask a few questions:

- Did the teacher clarify the aim or objective of the lesson?
- Did the steps or activities align with that objective?
- Did the lesson include an assessment of what students had learned?
- Did the teacher make any effort to monitor learning—that is, to check for understanding or reteach even once during the lesson?

Several of my colleagues began to acknowledge that these lessons needed a lot of work and that the university's evaluation tool was nearly useless. Its dizzying array of criteria had diverted their focus from the core elements of an effective lesson.

Soon after, I was asked to do occasional presentations in a program for working teachers and administrators from abroad. This was at a highly ranked education school. The participants were receptive to my attempts to describe, demonstrate, and coach them in the elements of an effective lesson, but none of it took. Those brief experiences were overridden, before and after, by months of learning anything but how to teach effectively.

At the end of the program, I was invited to observe their culminating assessment—their delivery of a model lesson. The lessons, alas, were more like PowerPoint presentations, devoid of the elements of effective teaching. It was particularly depressing to listen to the gushing praise the lessons received from the program's full-time professors. These students had traveled thousands of miles to spend a semester learning the best the United States had to offer, but they never got the chance to master any version of explicit instruction.

Around this time, I was invited to participate as an occasional observer and co-instructor in a teaching methods course. My partner's sessions consisted of a variety of group activities, games, and informal chats. On the first night I was given the reins, I conducted a demonstration lesson and enjoined the class to role-play as my students. My partner was mystified. "You're actually teaching them *how to teach*," she said afterward. That professor went on to become the dean of an education school.

These experiences—along with conversations with several education school leaders and deans—confirmed my perception that preparation programs hadn't improved since my undergraduate years.

Clueless in Academe

My attempts to share such concerns with deans and department heads at multiple universities were always a little awkward (Schmoker, 2019c). These leaders were hard-working, conscientious people, but most seemed oblivious to the contradiction at the heart of teacher education—between the reverential references to research and the general failure to ensure that students master evidence-based instructional methods.

I would begin these conversations by gently probing to see how familiar they were with the research on curriculum, literacy, and effective instruction. In every case, they were familiar with it and would concede its veracity. However, when I asked if the coursework at their institutions addressed these elements, they avoided direct answers. I would then share with them that their graduates routinely told me they had not learned about the indispensable importance of curriculum or about the urgent need for large daily amounts of reading, writing, and writing instruction. Some of their graduates had acquired a cursory knowledge of instruction and its terminology, but they hadn't learned its supportive research or how to execute an effective lesson.

One official, after acknowledging the importance of the research on explicit instruction, told me that it should be the school's responsibility, not the college's, to provide such training— in professional development. She didn't provide any rationale for this, nor did she share my concern that university-based preservice establishes the pattern for professional development, which, in turn, neglects to train teachers in these core elements.

At another school of education, I asked a department head and acquaintance if his university was addressing the chronic absence of curriculum in most schools. He was incredulous. For all the academic papers he had published, he was unaware that "curricular chaos" was the rule rather than the exception in most school districts. It was gratifying to run into him later, after he had begun to read up on this issue and visit schools. He now saw these problems vividly.

At one of these universities, several officials and graduates encouraged me to take my queries to an assistant dean of teacher preparation. Over lunch, she conceded that the basic components of structured instruction were crucial, but she expressed no concern whatsoever about graduates' complaints that they had barely been exposed to these components. She informed me that her department had different research priorities. She also went on to become the dean of a school of education in a neighboring state.

I'll end this section with a comment about a newspaper article I came across by the dean of a highly ranked teacher-training institution. After lamenting the "curse" of our enduring achievement gaps, the dean declared that the solution, and the new mission of the university, was to go all-in on . . . *personalized learning*. This was doubly ironic because that dean's university was among the founding members of Deans for Impact, an organization whose mission is to convince schools of education to abjure pedagogic fads and embrace only the best evidence-based principles of effective schooling. In addition, the founding head of Deans for Impact, Benjamin Riley (2017), regards personalized learning as precisely the sort of unproven, misconceived initiative his organization works to expose.

Happily, Riley is not alone among education professors calling out the inadequacies of teacher preparation. Many prominent professors and prestigious entities recognize that these programs are in crisis.

"Inadequate to Appalling"

The most damning indictments of preservice teacher training come from the most respected members in the profession. Arthur Levine is the former dean of the prestigious Teachers College at Columbia University. Few people have more authority to render judgment on our schools of education. In 2006, he spearheaded a comprehensive, four-year study of hundreds of programs.

"Teacher education," he writes, "is the Dodge City of the education world. Like the fabled Wild West town, it is unruly and chaotic." The profession lacks clear standards or criteria by which to evaluate its own effectiveness. Most programs are engaged in the "pursuit of irrelevance" and long ago exchanged evidence for (note the term) *ideology*. For these reasons, teacher and administrative preparation programs "range from inadequate to appalling, even at some of the country's leading universities" (Levine, 2006, p. 12). In the entire United States, Levine found only two programs that met basic standards for teacher preparation.

He reports that professors and administrators from other academic departments regard schools of education with scorn—as the "poorest quality units" on campus. Our only hope, he writes, is "transforming teacher preparation as we know it" (Stevens, 2015, para. 4). Further, he recommends we shut down unproductive programs and convert the best ones that remain into professional schools focused on classroom practice (Levine, 2006).

Ponder the implications of such conclusions. This might be akin to the head of a major U.S. automaker declaring, "We typically make hopelessly inferior cars." In conducting his study, Levine discovered that those in charge of these programs recoiled at the prospect of "truth telling." They were less interested in reforming their departments than in urging Levine to publish a defense of the status quo. Fortunately, some of the most prominent among the education school professoriate are keen on truth telling. A growing number now acknowledge findings such as Levine's. In anonymous surveys, sizeable proportions now concede that their programs don't prepare teachers for their work (Stevens, 2015).

Lyell Asher (2019), a former University of Virginia professor, pulls no punches in commenting on these studies. These programs are tainted by "ideological orthodoxy and low academic standards" and have thus become "a menace to higher education." He discovered that broad swathes of education faculties admit that the coursework they provide is "subjective, obscure, faddish . . . inbred, and politically correct" (para. 8).

Linda Darling-Hammond is among the most frequently cited education scholars. She delineates the essential criteria that distinguish a true profession. First, its practitioners must acquire a rigorous common knowledge base and know how to employ it. Second, its members must "take responsibility for defining, transmitting, and enforcing standards of practice to protect" their clients. On these bases, however, she concludes that education "has not yet acquired" professional status (Darling-Hammond, 2020, para. 4).

Robert Pianta, former dean of the School of Education at the University of Virginia, found that a degree in education isn't strongly linked to effective teaching. Like Levine, he's dismayed that his colleagues resist admitting this. They also resisted having their programs evaluated when the Obama Administration proposed doing so. "I am embarrassed," writes Pianta, "that professionals responsible for the preparation of teachers seem to oppose so adamantly efforts to evaluate the competence of the workforce they produce" (Stevens, 2015, para. 2).

David Steiner is executive director of the Johns Hopkins Institute for Education Policy, a professor of education, and the former New York State commissioner of education. He believes there should be consequences for education schools' resistance to reform. He would have states deny accreditation to programs that don't ensure prospective educators learn the best evidence-based teaching methods (Pondiscio, 2014).

Multiple organizations also affirm the perceptions of these esteemed educators and are calling for fundamental reforms.

The Courageous Speak Out

As the evidence mounts, the problems with schools of education are impossible to deny. As I noted earlier, Eric Kalenze, one of the founders of ResearchED, dubs the state of our current system as "upside down"—in an oppositional relationship to proven practice. The National Council for Accreditation of Teacher Education (NCATE) believes the enterprise should be redesigned from beginning to end to ensure educators both know and can implement high-leverage teaching methods. NCATE (2010) urges a recognition that

> Teaching, like medicine, is a profession of practice, and prospective teachers must be prepared to become expert practitioners who know how to use the knowledge of their profession to advance student learning . . . through practice. In order to achieve this, we must place practice at the center of teacher preparation. (p. 2)

The problem with our education schools, as any teacher will tell you, is that practical training, with mastery as its goal, is precisely what is absent from their programs. That's why NCATE calls for us to emulate medicine, a profession in which practitioners learn their practice *through* practice. There is no other way.

The National Council on Teacher Quality (NCTQ) conducted another large-scale study of U.S. teacher education programs (Greenberg, McKee, & Walsh, 2013). An overwhelming majority of the nation's 1,450 schools of education participated. The study found that only a small number of schools of education prepare their graduates for their work. Many years after his own study was conducted, Arthur Levine affirmed NCTQ's conclusions, remarking that perhaps no other profession provides less adequate preparation for its aspirants

(Sawchuck, 2013). Deans for Impact, as well, is calling for schools of education to reorient their efforts around solid evidence and to take a stand against pervasive malpractice and unproven educational fads (Riley, 2017).

In light of such heavy, perennial criticism, we might hope that serious improvements would be underway, but as *Education Week*'s Katherine Stevens (2015) points out, "Real reform is still nowhere in sight." Why? It's because of the peculiar but entrenched "culture of education," which is informed by ideologies that reject the very notion of proven practices or the need to provide training in them.

The Root Cause of the Problem: The Culture of Education

Education professor Mark Seidenberg's (2017) work in the area of literacy has received high praise—along with his critique of undergraduate teacher preparation. He uses the term the *culture of education* to refer to the operational assumptions of "the educators who teach the teachers." Seidenberg warns us that his appraisal may seem harsh to readers, but such candor is in order because this culture is truly "an obstacle to improving educational outcomes." Why? Its dominant beliefs and practices aren't rooted in evidence; they're rooted in "ideology" (p. 249).

What is ideology? It's a set of related beliefs or theories that are insufficiently substantiated by empirical evidence. Moreover, some educational ideologies are tenaciously embraced in proportion to the *lack* of such evidence.

It should concern us, as Seidenberg (2017) maintains, that the principal function of schools of education isn't to ensure that graduates learn to employ evidence-based practices. On the contrary, their function is to "socialize prospective teachers into an ideology" (p. 251). In his use of the term, he joins a host of critics. For E. D. Hirsch (2020), "The education of our teachers today is determined more by ideology and personal predilection than the needs of our children" (p. 96).

David Steiner and Susan Rozen studied 16 representative schools of education. They discovered that the overriding mission of these institutions wasn't to equip teachers to teach well. Rather, it was to advance popular but amorphous "ideologies"—such as helping teachers develop their "professional identities" (Seidenberg, 2017, p. 253). Some of education's dominant ideologies are grounded in the theoretical work of Jerome Bruner, John Dewey, Lev Vygotsky, Jean Piaget, and their protégés. They have canonical status in schools of education, although the evidence supporting them hardly warrants the priority they're given. As Seidenberg (2017) writes, "Reality bites." Among the first discoveries teachers make when they enter the classroom "is the irrelevance of most of the theory they learned." Despite being steeped in theory, "teachers are left to discover effective classroom practices" on their own "because they haven't been taught them" (p. 255).

Diminishing Expectations

We have a professional obligation to warn teachers of the limitations of the work of Dewey, Bruner, Vygotsky, and Piaget. Many of their postulations have been superseded by subsequent research, and they often inform practices that are insupportable. For instance, Dewey's theories, which were not subjected to rigorous testing, emphasized "active learning"—that is, engaging the mind and the body during the school day. However, he stressed this to an extreme, and (as we'll see) at the expense of literacy. His belief that knowledge must be individually "constructed" by students in their own time led us to place excessive faith in self-directed "discovery" or independent "project-based" learning.

As Seidenberg (2017) observes, these have their place. However, few prospective teachers are ever taught that for these approaches to work, they have "to be closely coupled to explicit guidance and instruction" (p. 255). Dewey's work inspired generations of teachers to deride explicit, whole-class instruction as feckless "sage on the stage" teaching. Ironically, this mischaracterization deprived them of their most powerful tool for promoting each individual's capacity to discover and construct their own knowledge, to work with increasing success on independent assignments and projects.

The work of Bruner and Vygotsky abetted this overemphasis on the unique needs and developmental stages of individual learners. Bruner's experiments demonstrated that each child's idiosyncratic sociocultural makeup determined what and how they could learn. This led to unfounded extrapolations—for example, that children must be taught differently because each child is affected by a complex web of such factors. Likewise, Vygotsky placed inordinate emphasis on the importance of assessing, then addressing, each child's social context (Risko, as cited in Seidenberg, 2017). As we've seen, though, the most high-leverage, whole-class practices generate dramatic gains in schools serving students from a variety of cultures.

As Daniel Willingham (2019) takes pains to demonstrate, ideological statements such as "learning is social," "everybody learns differently," or "knowledge is constructed" are not grounded in empirical evidence. They are ideologies—and open to multiple interpretations. We should not conflate them with clear, specific, proven practices.

The work of Jean Piaget is similarly problematic. He insisted that students can only learn according to fixed stages of cognitive development consistent with individuals' "developmental levels." This term became a mantra for those wishing to justify diminished academic expectations, which has had an especially devastating effect on poor and marginalized students. Piaget generally underestimated students' intellectual capacity and discounted the decisive contribution that effective teaching can make to the acceleration of learning (Crossland, 2015).

Few practitioners ever learn that students routinely learn things that would be impossible if Piaget's theories were accurate (Willingham, 2019). He was a theoretician whose work has fallen out of favor among many serious scientists (Hopkins, 2011). Nevertheless, these theories continue to get trotted out to justify low expectations. One education scholar recently cited Piaget in calling for the abolition of even the most reasonable, achievable grade-level expectations, such as expecting a 2nd grader to understand and write the equation 2 + 2 = 4 (in McKibben, 2020).

The culture of preservice lends such theories more respect than they deserve. I don't know of any cases where their application resulted in substantial gains in learning. If anything, they furnish a rationale for practices that hold students back—especially in the area of literacy.

Literacy—Gutted by Ideology

Dewey's theories include surprisingly disparaging thoughts on literacy. He didn't think students should be taught to read or write until at least the age of 8. He regarded linguistic skills as mere "arbitrary tasks." As Diane Ravitch (2000) points out, Dewey believed that "reading itself was overvalued" and advanced the "bizarre idea that the need for reading and writing was decreasing as society advanced" (p. 357). We can see the legacy of his work in the paucity of reading, writing, and writing instruction in our schools, perhaps the greatest blight on the school day. Dewey's antiliterate legacy may have contributed to one of the most bizarre developments in decades: the call by the National Council of Teachers of English to give less emphasis—not more—to books and expository writing (Schmoker, 2022).

Let's now consider Vygotsky's popular concept of the zone of proximal development, which dictates that students learn best when the learning task is within their just-right range or "zone" of difficulty. There are problems with this concept. Educator David Didau cites numerous literacy experts to point up the "amorphous" nature of the concept. For literacy expert Annemarie Palincsar, it is "one of the most used and least understood constructs to appear in contemporary educational literature" (in Didau, 2017, para. 3).

Like so many such ideologies, it encouraged teachers to expect less from capable, and especially marginalized, students. It contributed directly to our use of increasingly less-challenging "leveled" reading tasks and books. As literacy expert Timothy Shanahan (2014) makes clear, students acquire more knowledge, vocabulary, and critical reading skills from grade-level reading materials than from banal, controlled-vocabulary leveled texts. These decelerate learning—and eliminate any hope of helping students catch up to grade-level peers. This is especially important in a time of pandemic-related learning loss. When teachers carefully scaffold literacy instruction, students routinely make rapid strides by completing tasks and reading texts well above their (supposed) zone of proximal development.

In addition, the exaggerated emphasis on each child's just-right zone discourages efficient, whole-class teaching. Remember, students receive at least *three times as much instruction* when we rely more heavily on whole-group than small-group teaching or tutoring (Schmoker, 2019a). Every highly effective teacher I have known uses small groups sparingly. They provide structured, whole-class lessons followed by limited, strategic tutoring or small-group assistance.

The many schools cited in these chapters prove the effectiveness of this approach. Faculty at Brockton High School succeeded because they went all-in on common, challenging curricula combined with abundant amounts of reading, writing, and whole-class structured instruction. As Principal Susan Szachowicz told me, the leadership team resisted suggestions from those who urged them to differentiate instruction. That's why the school made the largest gains in Massachusetts in a single year and then rose from the lowest-achieving 1 percent of schools to the top 10 percent five years later.

For all this, educators continue to implement and justify their use of inferior practices on the basis of unsubstantiated theories and ideologies. The harm they inflict continues to hide from all of us within the cosseted, insular culture of schools of education.

Out of Touch and Misaligned

Parents, writes Seidenberg (2017), "make a big mistake" in trusting that their children's teachers have been taught how to teach effectively (p. 249). Likewise, teachers and administrators also make a big mistake when they assume the theories that emanate from preservice programs are based on evidence. Within the wider university, education departments have become isolated from the more empirical sciences.

For Seidenberg (2017), they now "inhabit an academic island, cut off from other disciplines and well defended against incursions. The barriers between educational training programs and related sciences . . . are especially well entrenched" (p. 249). This isolation is so severe that some suggest universities should force the integration of education departments into other science departments to ensure they meet more legitimate academic and empirical standards.

Most K–12 practitioners aren't aware of this crisis of legitimacy. They wouldn't guess that prominent education professors, like Harvard's Jal Mehta, believe the shoddy standards and practices of U.S. education schools constitute "a failed profession" (Seidenberg, 2017, p. 250).

As Seidenberg (2017) writes, this failure translates into teacher and administrative preparation that is "misaligned with children's needs." Indeed, the very "people who enter the field of education" are themselves betrayed by this misalignment; they are "underserved by the authorities they have entrusted with their careers" (p. 249). Again, nothing changes because teachers and administrators aren't aware of this execrable misalignment. We can't fight what we can't see. For these reasons, Seidenberg is convinced that schools won't improve until we end the schools of education's "hegemony over education" (p. 249).

With the right reforms, these institutions *could* save our schools. For now, though, their program priorities stand athwart the development of what classroom teachers need most: a clear, codified body of evidence-based principles and practices.

No Right Way to Teach—Really?

In my doctoral studies, I took education courses from professors with national reputations. The most prominent scoffed at the suggestion that we could identify evidence-based practices. They believed, as Elmore (1999–2000) observed, that instruction is "an idiosyncratic and mysterious process that varies with each teacher" (p. 16).

The prevailing ethos, writes Seidenberg (2017), is that "education [that is, teaching practice] can't be codified [empirically identified and prioritized] like law or medicine." That postmodern ethos purports that learning is a "culturally determined construct that is always in flux"—subject to complex combinations of social and individual factors and context (p. 250).

As a professor once said to me, never use the word *should* about any teaching practice. For him, there were no right ways to teach—only ways that work for individual teachers with individual students in particular situations.

As Robert Pondiscio (2014) tells us,

> [Education professors] dare not suggest that there is a right (or wrong) way to teach. Anything that might reduce a teacher's latitude and ability to make professional choices in the context of each unique classroom is off the table. (para. 4)

However, as John Hattie's extensive research demonstrates, there are indeed *"right ways,* across all curricular domains to promote the acquisition of knowledge, deeper understanding, greater curiosity and fun in learning. We are surrounded by evidence of what works best. And yet, we still flail around with weak strategies, or *continue to implement that which suits us"* (in Schmoker, 2018).

Our failure to codify and impart the most vital proven practices to educators degrades teachers' self-efficacy by depriving them of powerful pedagogic tools that build professional confidence and that multiply the number of students whose lives they truly affect. This failure also promotes teacher anxiety and confusion about how to do their job well (Buckingham, 2005). In the absence of clear, established practices, "we have teachers essentially winging it as they go along" (Mehta, as cited in Seidenberg, 2017, p. 250). They are left to discover effective classroom practices on their own because they haven't been taught them. This Wild West culture accounts for why an unnecessarily large proportion of students

- Do arts and crafts in English and social studies.
- Seldom learn from vocabulary-rich grade-level text.
- Rarely engage in intellectually robust discussions.

- Graduate without learning to write clear, cogent prose.
- Struggle or fail in math and science courses, where failure rates are highest.
- Reach high school but read at an elementary level.

These consequences of a "failed profession" are also buffered; they're out of sight of the average, trusting education school student. The failure to codify—to acknowledge the most indispensable instructional practices—has another consequence: It absolves preservice programs of their duty to provide practical training in essential pedagogic skills. The buffer hides education's cultural aversion to such training.

The Failure to Train

"Training," writes Robert Pondiscio (2014), "is 'a dirty word' in teacher preparation institutions. A majority of programs studiously avoid any content that suggests that their role is to 'train' teacher candidates" (para. 5). In the main, writes Seidenberg (2017), "Prospective teachers aren't trained to teach" (p. 250). There's an abiding prejudice against training in preservice, against providing teachers with opportunities to practice essential methods under the guidance of experts. This failure to train is among the most dismaying features of preservice preparation. Addressing it may be the most propitious but overlooked opportunity for substantial improvements to instruction.

I never received meaningful training in any of my coursework, right up through my doctoral studies. Why? For starters, you can't confidently train people in a profession that won't acknowledge there are right and wrong ways to teach—that certain practices are so effective that all practitioners should learn and implement them. This lets education departments off the hook, free to pursue whatever research agenda they prefer, while ignoring the need to equip teachers with the skills they need to impart knowledge and intellectual skills to their students.

Many in the university regard training with condescension. Arthur McKee, one of the lead authors of the NCTQ report on the woeful state of teacher preparation, notes that the "dominant ethos" of teacher preparation institutions "is opposed to training as a mission," regarding it as a "low prestige" activity (in Pondiscio, 2014).

Here, for instance, is a prominent education dean expressing her disdain for an alternative program that trains teachers in powerful instructional methods:

> What they are doing is teacher training. . . . And I think that what that does is it dumbs down teaching and takes us back a few steps, in terms of our struggle in the profession for teachers to be seen as professionals. (Otterman, 2011, sec. 3, para. 15)

Thank God such scorn doesn't prevail in medicine.

Training is conspicuously low on the agenda of the most prestigious educational organizations, such as the venerable American Educational Research Association (AERA). They now proclaim that methods courses should cease to focus on "particular methods of instruction." Instead—cue the ideology—we should reconceive them as "complex and unique sites" where "teachers' beliefs, teaching practices, and creation of identities" should be explored. They *reject the need* to create a "training environment in which specific strategies are transmitted and practiced" (Seidenberg, 2017, p. 251).

Does the public or do school-based educators know that many education professors recoil at the prospect of equipping our teachers with the most vital instructional strategies? My professors couldn't have imagined themselves as trainers. Their scholarly aspirations ran to wide-ranging philosophical issues. Significantly, I never heard any of them acknowledge the need for better instruction in our schools. This wasn't their concern or their research interest.

This dominant ethos of teacher education denies most U.S. teachers the personal and professional rewards that teachers in other countries enjoy.

Everywhere but Here

Teacher preparation is radically different in high-achieving nations. As bestselling author James Surowiecki (2014) writes, profound improvements have occurred in numerous spheres as a result of a "rev-olution" around intense, practical training. Schools in Japan, Finland, and Canada "take training seriously." They "train teachers rigorously before they enter the classroom," and they've seen their educational performance soar commensurately. However, "in one area above all," the failure to embrace training "is especially egregious: [U.S.] educa-tion." Surowiecki believes this accounts for why U.S. achievement has "barely budged" over the decades (paras. 21–23).

Still, there's hope for our schools if we can learn from the best mod-els. Sharon Otterman (2011), writing for *The New York Times*, cites the Relay Graduate School of Education, founded by Norman Atkins and Doug Lemov, creators of the exceptionally high-achieving UnCommon Schools network. Unlike typical preparation programs, Relay doesn't dodge its obligation to codify, prioritize, and thoroughly train teachers in effective practices. Its graduates are coached to mastery in high-leverage techniques—in "the stuff that will help you be a better teacher on Monday" (p. 4).

Relay is light on the likes of Dewey, Piaget, and Vygotsky: the "canon of intellectuals that tend to take up an outsize portion" of tra-ditional preservice (Otterman, 2011, para. 27). Brent Maddin is Relay's senior manager of teaching and learning. As he told Otterman, people who want to know how to shoe a horse don't need to learn a ton of the-ory from books. They mostly need to be shown how to shoe horses and practice doing so under the guidance of an expert. For Atkins, schools won't improve until we move beyond ideology—from mere theory to genuine training in proven methods.

When ideology trumps training in sound methodology, our teach-ers leave their preparation programs with no idea how to effectively instruct a classroom of children (Green, 2010).

Preparation That Doesn't Prepare

"The most damning testimony" of education programs, writes Elizabeth Green (2010), "comes from the graduates." She describes a teacher who took all the usual education courses, including (so-called) teaching methods; the history of education; and courses on race, culture, and class. She also completed a full semester of student teaching, but when she entered her first classroom, she realized she had no idea how to teach her students.

Ask any first-year teacher, and they will tell you, "Nothing prepared me for my first year as a teacher" (Pondiscio, 2014). No one, adds Pondiscio, would tolerate doctors who learned to do bypass surgery only from books, largely by themselves, through trial and error, on unsuspecting patients—and *only after* they were fully licensed to practice medicine.

Nevertheless, that's the situation most new teachers find themselves in, a fact confirmed by virtually every major study (Stevens, 2015). It's why the National Council for Accreditation of Teacher Education (2010) describes educational preparation as so misconceived that it "needs to be turned upside down . . . redesigned from beginning to end" around practical training. They call for an acknowledgment that "teaching, like medicine, is a profession of practice" (p. 2).

Consider a study by a superintendent and an assistant superintendent, Gary Chesley and Janice Jordan (2012). Over the years, they watched scores of beginning teachers struggle in their district. Their new teachers came from 17 different universities, and the administrators discovered that the coursework in these various preservice programs was simply not useful in actual schools. As a result, they call for radical retooling of preparation programs around practical classroom realities.

In numerous focus group sessions, the teachers told Chesley and Jordan that they arrived at their schools with no practical experience in formative assessment or checks for understanding, that they didn't learn to teach content, and that they didn't learn to plan for instruction. No one taught them how to conduct all-important purposeful discourse. Before their first teaching positions, they never actually presented lessons to expert trainers or coaches for feedback.

Finally, let's consider two Minnesota teachers who received their degrees from two well-known teacher training programs. In "Training

Teachers to Fail" (Lane & Gustafson, 2020), they inform us that they didn't receive much purposeful practice in their teacher training. Instead, they were ceaselessly encouraged to give minimal guidance to students and to emphasize student choice—and the integration of technology into lessons. "Oddly enough," they write, "we were not trained in *how to actually teach*" (p. 3). They didn't learn about the necessity for students to acquire robust background knowledge in social studies, science, and the arts, and no one taught them how to teach expository writing. The sum of their coursework "felt more like a philosophy of teaching degree" than a teacher preparation program (para. 9).

They write just as scathingly of their student teaching experience. Both were told they "shouldn't be at the front of the room" when their university supervisor came to observe them. Good thing, as they received "minimal to nonexistent training in effective whole-group instruction." In sum, they submit they "were not prepared for the responsibility of the job," and they take pains to point to the consequences of the kind of pseudopreparation provided to teachers in their state. Indeed, Minnesota has the widest reading gap in the United States between white and nonwhite students (Lane & Gustafson, 2020, paras 2–6).

It is worth repeating: Preparation programs could change this and have a decisive effect on teaching and learning—maybe more than any other part of the system. It's the first stop on a teacher's career path, when they are eager to learn essential competencies and have the time to acquire them in their coursework.

"Weakest Link"—Or Richest Opportunity?

Nearly every teacher I've spoken with agrees with these assessments of preparation programs. That leaves us, paradoxically, in an exquisite situation:

- High learning and literacy rates depend enormously on good teaching.

- Good teaching depends on competent training in effective teaching methods.
- Training is typically lacking in preservice programs.
- If prospective teachers *did* receive effective training, student learning would soar.

Our schools of education could begin to transform schooling by providing just one well-taught methods course. The effect on students would be magnified by every new teacher who entered their first schools to teach with the confidence that can only come with practice-based training.

This doesn't mean that improvement must wait until schools of education make essential reforms. There's another reliable source of school transformation: on-the-job professional development. Done right, it can compensate for the deficiencies of preservice teacher education. That's the subject of the next chapter.

How to Promote Practical Teacher Training: Action Questions for Leaders

- Have you ever had doubts about the value of or evidence base for some of the prominent theories you learned in education courses?
- What practical, essential training, in specific practices, do you wish you had received in your coursework
  —As an undergraduate?
  —As a prospective administrator?
- How can schools and districts effectively convey their need for such specific, practical training
  —To the universities that prepare their teachers?
  —To the universities that prepare their administrators?

7

Why Professional Development "Almost Always Sucks"

Most professional development is lousy.

—Valerie Strauss

Standard-issue professional development (PD) is lamentable. It's mired in erroneous notions that often originate in our teacher preparation institutions. Done right, it could transform schooling. Here again, the good (indeed the best) news is that the shortcomings are proportional to the opportunity—and PD's shortcomings are *gargantuan*.

Like so much in our K–12 system, it's "upside down." It's not driven by evidence but by unproven fads and fashionable theories. That's why it has had so little positive effect on teaching and learning.

Let's look at the two most damning facts about typical PD:

- It **hasn't reduced** the most common, indefensible forms of malpractice—for example, the paucity of reading and writing, the predominance of worksheets, the aimless and excessive group work, and curricular chaos.
- It **hasn't increased** the implementation of the most essential and effective practices. Only a tiny minority of schools implement

the most crucial elements of good schooling described in Chapters 2–4 (on the fundamentals of curriculum, literacy, and effective instruction).

A few years ago, The New Teacher Project (TNTP, 2015) published the landmark study *The Mirage: Confronting the Hard Truth about Our Quest for Teacher Development.* The study's central finding was that despite our massive investment in PD, its benefits are illusory. The researchers found that the 50 largest U.S. school districts spend more than $8 billion each year on PD, and yet in the districts the researchers studied, teacher effectiveness had either stagnated or *declined* over a three-year period. There was no significant effect on instructional practice or student outcomes. Revealingly, most teachers interviewed for the study considered professional development a waste of time.

Decades of studies confirm these findings. PD often fails because it avoids a focus on the most crucial elements of good schooling, and, like preservice, it shuns practical training. Countless observers, such as those that follow, have called out its enormous shortcomings:

- Yvette Jackson spent a career in teacher education and was the director of professional development for New York City schools. "What teachers need to improve their practice," she notes, "is rarely what they receive from professional development" (in Strauss, 2011, para. 5). As examples, she cites Los Angeles Unified Schools, whose $500 million investment in staff development turned out to be largely ineffective in raising student performance. Another initiative, a 12-district, 2-year math improvement program, had no measurable impact on achievement (Strauss, 2011).
- The work of team-based professional learning communities is an essential form of PD, but effective teams are exceedingly rare. Instead of focusing on developing and refining lessons on the basis of assessment results, team meetings routinely devolve into loosely structured discussions that have no effect on student outcomes (Ermeling & Graff-Ermeling, 2016).

- Valerie Strauss (2014a), an education writer for *The Washington Post*, reports that "most professional development for teachers is useless." It's so bad that teachers are "going out of their minds." She describes teachers in Chicago being led through activities that insult their intelligence and waste their time. "This only confirms," writes Strauss, "what is well known in the education world: most professional development is lousy." Strauss references a study by the National School Boards Association that found that most PD is "nothing short of abysmal." The study cites former secretary of education Arne Duncan's opinion that it's "largely a waste." Teachers themselves consider PD to be "a foolhardy waste of valuable time and money" (paras. 1–3).
- Alvin Crawford (Strauss, 2014b), a 20-year veteran in the field of PD, notes that there are "huge problems with professional development." Most of it is "totally useless" in helping teachers improve their craft. "No one can argue," he adds, "with this conclusion" (paras. 7–8).
- Robert Pondiscio (2021b) notes that we need to know two things about PD. First, it's almost never focused on helping teachers teach what they need to teach; second, the quality "almost always sucks" (para. 1).

Like university preservice preparation, PD's agenda is not driven by science or evidence. It's more often driven by hucksterism—by the aggressive marketing of books and conference presentations on high-sounding but unproven pedagogic fads like those we've discussed. It's also ineffective because it rarely includes real training—that is, demonstration, practice, and follow-up opportunities that would enable practitioners to actually master the most essential instructional methods (Strauss, 2014a).

No Training, No Practice

I once sat among a group of high school math teachers attending a mandatory, all-district PD session on the Common Core State Standards for math. They eagerly anticipated what every teacher deserves: clarity on what math concepts to teach and guidance on how to teach them.

All they got were presentation slides and vague generalizations from the full-time district professional developer, who appeared to have no idea how to implement these new standards. The teachers' questions were met with unhelpful assertions taken verbatim from the abstruse language of the Common Core and its promotional materials.

Those teachers had come to this session in hopes of learning something they could apply in the classroom. They got nothing of the sort, and they never received any training whatsoever. They never watched a demonstration lesson or even a portion of one; they were never given a chance, under expert guidance, to practice with the new standards. No one's practice changed.

More recently, I provided weeks of complimentary consulting to a school district. It focused on simplifying their teacher evaluation system around a few simple elements of teaching. The central office was excited and could see this would have a salutary effect on instructional quality. Then the district PD team got hold of it. With good intentions, they began to add to the simple, straightforward model. They kept incorporating new elements that they illustrated with confusing graphs, arrows, boxes, and labels. Instead of training with demonstrations, teacher modeling, and coaching, faculty were subjected to slideshow presentations. I eventually heard that the initiative had no effect on teaching practices.

Typical PD continues to avoid identifying best practices and training teachers until they acquire basic mastery. When teachers receive such PD, reinforced in team-based professional learning communities, they will absolutely begin to see results almost immediately—in days or weeks.

Instead, teacher "training" typically consists of superficial presentations on one or another educational fad or mandate, often based on a new or an attractive theory. This has been the case for decades. Like preservice "training," PD still prefers fads and ideology to science-based practice and training.

Ideology Versus Empiricism

I know a thriving PD organization that emphatically claims to embrace evidence-based practice. Its founder is a rightly respected researcher. You would think that people in this organization would ground their services, workshops, and materials in the best of that research.

Not necessarily. A spokesperson for the group recently celebrated the new dawn, in which we have moved past the bad old days of "teacher-centered instruction." We now know, the spokesperson added, that students don't need explicit instructional guidance. They must be liberated to "lead their own learning."

These are fatuous assertions. They distort the best research of the organization's founder. As that work conclusively demonstrates, students need liberal amounts of guidance to learn. They need large helpings of explicit instruction to successfully lead their own learning, to complete independent projects and assignments (Seidenberg, 2017).

The PD industry characteristically proclaims such nonsense with impunity; it ignores or disparages the essential ingredients of successful schooling. It represents the triumph of expedience, commercialism, and sentimentality over science.

Whims, Fads, Opportunism— And Yes, More Ideology

In Chapter 5, we looked at some major educational initiatives, such as new teacher evaluation schemes, the Common Core State Standards, and educational technology. As we saw, none of these is supported by solid research, and none has had any substantial positive effect on student learning. This didn't prevent them from supplanting the most urgently needed professional development initiatives.

These expensive, large-scale initiatives dominated PD for decades, but dozens of other unproven and ephemeral (often recycled or renamed) initiatives emerge annually. Over the years, I have come across or attended workshops on such topics as

- "Literacy-based" craft activities using milk cartons and craft sticks
- Standards-based grading
- Teacher efficacy
- Blended learning
- The flipped classroom
- Student podcasts
- "Effortful thinking"
- Using social media in instruction
- Integrating TikTok into lessons
- Promoting student engagement
- Classroom strategies for encouraging "out of the box thinking"
- Cognitive mapping
- Promoting student voice and choice

Feel free to think that some of these have potential value, but no evidence proves that any of these belong on any list of the most vital, effective practices. We simply can't compare them with the high-leverage, evidence-based practices I discussed in Chapters 2 through 4.

It makes no sense to provide professional development for such initiatives when the majority of our schools have yet to provide their teachers with a coherent curriculum; when teachers have never been thoroughly trained in the most powerful teaching methods (such as "checking for understanding"); when they haven't been taught how to teach analytic reading, how to conduct productive discussions, or how to teach students to write clearly and effectively in math, music, English, art, and science.

Nothing will change until we implore PD providers to build their programs around these priorities. It should deeply disturb us that PD providers are simply "not members of an evidence-based community." On the contrary, research reveals that professional development has operated, for decades, on the basis of "whims, fads, opportunism, and ideology" (Corcoran, Fuhrman, & Belcher, 2001, p. 80).

What We Stand to Lose—Or Gain

What are the net results of perpetuating the current K–12 system—and what do we forfeit?

- We get teacher frustration, cynicism, and turnover. We deny teachers the professional satisfaction and sense of competence they deserve.
- We waste hundreds of school hours every year.
- We bore, frustrate, and fail to engage students in intellectually stimulating learning activities that prepare them for their personal and professional futures.
- We forfeit the chance to profoundly reduce opportunity gaps between rich and poor, between white students and students of color.
- We fail to cultivate the life of the mind—to produce literate, articulate, informed, and contributive citizens.
- We fail to ensure a decent standard of living for the 50 million students who walk into our schools every day.

I hope that the many scholars, studies, and schools cited here convince you that the opportunity to change this exhausted, irrational system is within reach. It's as close as our willingness to confront our shortcomings and replace poor practices with the best ones we know.

We have a duty to do this.

In the final chapter, we'll look at practical ways we can begin the effort and build momentum, one evidence-based action at a time.

How to Ensure Effective PD: Action Questions for Leaders

- It's well established that we cannot afford to focus on more than one or two improvement initiatives at a time and expect success (Buckingham, 2005; Collins, 2001). In light of that,

- — Does your school or district truly embrace the principle of priority? That is, does it conduct a meticulous study of the evidence to determine which initiatives would have the greatest effect on student learning?
- — Has your district PD department given due attention to the three crucial elements of curriculum, literacy, and effective instruction? Do they truly understand that a focus on these elements will have a greater effect on student achievement than all other factors combined? Are they aware that only a tiny fraction of our schools currently implement these practices?
- With colleagues, list and discuss professional development initiatives you've been involved with. How many of them
  - — Seemed, in retrospect, to be more fad-driven than evidence-based?
  - — Were accompanied by rigorous training that resulted in most teachers acquiring adequate mastery of proven, high-impact elements or methods?
  - — Had a positive and measurable payoff in student learning and literacy?
- What steps can you take to ensure that PD is, from now on, truly evidence-based and priority-driven?

8

How We Can Get Results—Now

People begin to feel the "magic of momentum"
when they begin to see tangible results.

—Jim Collins

Jim Collins (2001) couldn't be more emphatic. If an organization wishes to "make the leap" to greatness, there's only one place to begin: "You absolutely cannot make a series of good decisions without first confronting the brutal facts" (p. 70). We must "turn over rocks . . . even if what you see scares the hell out of you" (p. 72). Our greatest opportunities live under those rocks. The next step is for the "right people" to develop a "simple plan" that will deliver a continuous stream of "visible, tangible results" (p. 177). The best plans, writes Collins, are "remarkably simple and straightforward, even maddeningly so" (p. 68).

Some "Simple Plans"

Both school and systemwide improvement can start with anyone, anywhere and catch fire. Our goal should be the creation of an evidence-based, aligned system in which schools, universities, and government agencies reinforce one another's efforts to educate children effectively. Let's look at how these entities can help us achieve this goal.

Schools and School Districts

The first task of schools and school districts should be to courageously, even systematically, "confront the brutal facts" in the areas of curriculum, literacy, instruction, and instructional management. Every school district would benefit from conducting a curriculum audit, inclusive of a review of how much reading, discussion, writing, and writing instruction occurs during the school day. My audiences readily admit this would reveal a serious need for curriculum coherence—and oversight.

Schools should also conduct an instructional audit to compare current classroom practice with the evidence-based elements I described in Chapter 4: structured teaching, clear learning objectives, checks for understanding, reteaching, and a judicious use of group work and small-group instruction. Most schools will discover an alarming gap between classroom practice and what evidence reveals to have the greatest effect on student learning.

A curricular and an instructional audit will point us to our richest opportunities: the need to build a coherent, literacy-rich curriculum and provide practical, hands-on training in core instructional practices. Review the "how-to" sections at the end of Chapters 2–7 for more specific ideas on how to provide solid instructional management.

Professional Development and PLCs

Professional development must fully embrace these priorities, as well as its new goal: not seat time but at least approximate, initial mastery of effective teaching practices. This will be a radical shift for district and regional PD providers. If they accept this challenge, it will be the most productive change they have ever made.

To that end, schools must better define—and formalize—the work of professional learning communities (whose focus, alas, is prone to drift). As an essential arm of professional development, PLCs should have clear tasks and responsibilities to

- Equip teams of teachers to develop and continuously refine high-quality, literacy-rich curriculum with appropriate central office guidance.
- Master the core elements of effective teaching and employ them consistently.
- Collaboratively build and refine lessons and units together on the basis of assessment results.

Instructional Expertise

Schools and districts should give greater importance to the results of individual, successful lessons as the new unit by which to measure and celebrate improvement. Single-lesson "tangible results" could be the key to progress and transformation, to facilitating what Jim Collins calls the "flywheel effect" (2001).

The "Flywheel Effect"

Collins believes that progress hinges on our ability to generate and celebrate small but concrete accomplishments that align with carefully defined priorities. Once people are trained in a new strategy, leaders must capture and praise each achievable "tangible result" that contributes to the organization's primary goals. This enables others to see that the new strategy is effective, that it's vital to a valued goal, and that there's "monolithic unity" among leaders to sustain and reward effort toward that goal.

This basic plan powerfully overcomes resistance and creates a virtuous cycle as people gain confidence from the successes. This generates additional focused effort, as success and motivation compound and "people begin to feel the magic of momentum when they begin to see tangible results" (Collins, 2001, p. 177). Collins calls this the flywheel effect because, like a flywheel, each turn makes the next turn less effortful as the wheel gains momentum and increases in force.

Collins's metaphors are illuminating, but his basic elements affirm decades of findings about how successful organizations overcome resistance, sustain effort, and eventually achieve a breakthrough—the point at which effective practices become habitual and are producing superior, even spectacular results (Collins, 2001; Heath & Heath, 2011; Peters & Waterman, 1982; Schaffer, 1988). As Tom Peters writes, "The 'small, tangible steps' route to strategic breakthroughs is the only implementation strategy I know of that continually delivers dramatic results" (in Schaffer, 1988). Here's how schools can get there.

Share Measurable Results

Sharing measurable results from individual lessons can enable schools to "turn the flywheel" and produce dramatic results. Once a curriculum is in place—possibly before—leaders should urge PLC teams and teachers to collect data on even a single measurably successful lesson that demonstrates the effectiveness of structured instruction. A form such as the following might facilitate the effort:

> _____ (teacher/team) produced a lesson on _____ (e.g., applying one's knowledge of ratio and proportions to five real-world problems). They incorporated several cycles of checking for understanding and reteaching for each chunk of instruction. As a result, _____ (e.g., 29 of 32) students succeeded on the assessment (i.e., at least four of the five problems).

Principals would encourage these important efforts in the immediate wake of training and then share the measurable successes at faculty and district office meetings, as well as in district communications—anywhere they will inspire others and reinforce the power of high-leverage practices. If we sustained this simple regimen, if we filled the air with small successes, then it would powerfully animate instructional improvement.

Develop Effective Curricula

We would take a similar approach to curriculum development. Schools should celebrate, distribute, and have teachers examine and discuss the first curricula successfully completed by course-alike teams. These will demystify the curriculum-building process and provide models for others to emulate. (See Schmoker, 2018, pp. 46–52, for a more in-depth discussion of how to do this in a matter of hours.) Schools would celebrate each subsequent completion toward the goal: a coherent, literacy-rich curriculum for every course offered.

Spread the News

Schools should apprise their school boards and parents of these efforts. This is not an invitation to meddle or impose political agendas. It would merely provide what educators themselves tell me every parent is entitled to—an assurance that a high-quality curriculum is in place for every course their child takes and that the schools are availing themselves of the most effective, evidence-based teaching methods.

Parent nights would be excellent opportunities to showcase a sensible transparency concerning what goes on in their children's classes, to demonstrate our commitment to high-quality curriculum and instruction, and to share syllabi or course outlines with the assurance that these *accurately represent what their children will learn that year.* Such a "guaranteed curriculum" would increase trust and community support without the need for it to be fine grained (Marzano, 2003). It could be the most meaningful information parents have ever received. They would appreciate it.

Engage Regional Support

Federal, state, and county educational agencies could promote such transparency and alignment. Their "simple plan" could include developing what Michael Petrilli (2018) suggests—an "on track" metric, which, in addition to grades, would tell parents if their student is on track for college or a career. This would enable them to more effectively support their child's education, as well as the improvement of their local schools. It would also have a salutary effect on grading; it would encourage educational agencies to bring their grading in line with actual achievement levels.

These entities could also align their compliance regimens and funding with the curricular and instructional priorities described here. They could subsidize the development of coherent, literacy-rich curriculum models gathered within their jurisdictions and make them available online as models or templates. They could also provide incentives for districts to learn and implement the most powerful, evidence-based practices.

They could do the same for simple, priority-driven teacher evaluation templates. I would love to see these agencies fund district-based pilot projects to create seamless alignment among professional development, teacher evaluation, tenure, and compensation. Their curriculum models and teacher evaluation templates would focus primarily on two simple, reasonable criteria:

- The consistent delivery of a coherent, literacy-rich curriculum.
- Satisfactory and consistent implementation of the most high-leverage teaching practices (as described in Chapter 4).

Few educators are aware that such minimalist, priority-driven evaluation criteria are, in fact, the gold standard for promoting high performance (Buckingham, 2005; Goodwin, 2011). Teachers would thrive in such a priority-driven system, especially if educators made the case for these priorities when those prospective teachers were undergraduates.

Retool University-Based Preparation Programs

Preparation programs could have the most profoundly systemic effect on educational quality. A "simple plan" for preservice programs would include efforts to align at least some of their coursework with the most urgent needs of school districts in the areas of curriculum and instruction. Universities should partner with school districts or regional entities to more clearly establish and codify the most crucial competencies. With reasonable retooling, these programs could equip undergraduates with experience and capabilities in the following areas:

- **Curriculum:** Every preservice student would have opportunities to review and critique multiple samples of high-quality, full-year course curricula. As a course requirement, they would build a satisfactory curriculum with colleagues, replete with reading, discussion, and writing assignments (where appropriate). This would have a game-changing effect in this foundational area.

- **Literacy:** Every future K–12 teacher could acquire those simple, essential literacy abilities that apply across the curriculum, such as how to generate engaging questions about literature and subject-area content or how to lead a meaningful discussion in which all students participate (see Schmoker, 2018, pp. 140–142). They could acquire a serviceable ability to teach the basic moves of analyzing and writing about text—such as underlining and annotating, supporting a claim or argument with textual evidence, and developing a working outline for more formal writing assignments (see Schmoker, 2018, pp. 147–154).

- **Effective instruction:** With some retooling, programs could ensure that graduates leave school with a rudimentary ability to implement those few but powerful "routine components" of effective, explicit instruction I described in Chapter 4—offering structured teaching, developing clear learning objectives, checking for understanding, reteaching, and using group work and small-group instruction judiciously and sparingly (see Marzano, 2007, p. 180).

Imagine the effect on the entire system if every new teacher arrived at their first school with novice-level mastery in these core skills. To ensure this, teacher training institutions could more closely coordinate with schools to develop improved standards for student teaching so the experience supports (rather than undermines) evidence-based practice.

Finally, it's vital that universities exhort their charges to "do no harm." As a matter of professional responsibility, professors should inculcate, in the words of Harvard's Roland Barth (2002), an appropriate "moral outrage at ineffective practices." Teachers should learn about the most common but harmful time-wasting practices—a reliance on worksheets, excessive group work, and the "cut, color, and paste" activities that supplant authentic reading and writing instruction. Every graduate should know that these activities contribute directly to opportunity gaps, illiteracy, and reduced life chances for kids. A serious effort to impart a bone-deep aversion to such malpractice would reduce it appreciably.

These are reasonable expectations. If preparation programs met them, their effect would resonate in schools and classrooms with each new teacher's arrival, eventually transforming the system. Preservice programs could take pride in knowing their degrees reflect not course completion but essential instructional capabilities. Schools of education could—and this is admittedly aspirational—develop performance criteria by which to "certify" those graduates who demonstrate minimal proficiency in essential teaching skills.

The Time Is Now

Such straightforward reforms are well within reach of our schools and universities. The transformation must begin, however, with the first turn of the flywheel—an encounter with the brutal fact that "in education . . . we still don't wash our hands" (Willingham & Rotherham, 2020). If we're willing to take that first difficult step and follow it with the right actions, we could truly enter a golden age of education.

If we want it badly enough.

References

Allington, R. L. (2001). *What really matters for struggling readers*. Addison Wesley Longman.

Allington, R. L. (2011, March). What at-risk readers need. *Educational Leadership, 68*(6), 40–45.

Alter, C. (2014, September 22). 10 questions with Sheryl Sandberg. *Time.* https://time .com/3326567/10-questions-2

American Educator. (2010–2011, June). Common Core curriculum: An idea whose time has come. https://www.aft.org/sites/default/files/Editors_0.pdf

Anderson, J. (2012, February 19). States try to fix quirks in teacher evaluations. *The New York Times*. www.nytimes.com/2012/02/20/education/states-address-problems-with-teacher-evaluations.html

Anderson, R. C., Wilson, P. T., & Fielding, I. G. (1988). Growth in reading and how children spend their time outside of school. *Reading Research Quarterly, 2*(3), 285–303.

Asher, L. (2019, March 6). How ed schools became a menace to higher education. *Quillette*. https://quillette.com/2019/03/06/how-ed-schools-became-a-menace -to-higher-education

Azzam, A. (2008, March). Engaged and on track. *Educational Leadership, 65*(6), 93–94.

Bambrick-Santoyo, P., & Chiger, S. (2021, May 7). After the pandemic, schools can't hide from "learning loss." We must embrace it. *Newsweek*. www.newsweek.com/ after-pandemic-schools-cant-hide-learning-loss-we-need-embrace-it -opinion-1589545

Barber, M., & Fullan, M. (2005, March 1). Tri-level development. *Education Week*.

Barshay, J. (2020, March 30). Four things you need to know about the new reading wars. *Hechinger Report*. https://hechingerreport.org/four-things-you-need-to-know-about-the-new-reading-wars

Barth, R. (2002, May). The culture builder. *Educational Leadership, 59*(8), 6–11.

Bartlett, T. (2003, January 3). Why Johnny can't write, even though he went to Princeton. *Chronicle of Higher Education*. www.chronicle.com/article/why -johnny-cant-write-even-though-he-went-to-princeton

Barzun, J. (1991). *Begin here*. University of Chicago Press.

Bauerlein, M. (2009). *The dumbest generation: How the digital age stupefies young Americans and jeopardizes our future*. Jeremy P. Tarcher/Penguin.

Bennett, T. (2015, Spring). Group work for the good. *American Educator*. www.aft.org/ae/spring2015/bennett

Bergner, D. (2021, August 6). "White fragility" is everywhere. But does antiracism training work? *The New York Times Magazine*. www.nytimes.com/2020/07/15/magazine/white-fragility-robin-diangelo.html

Berliner, D. C. (1984). The half-full glass: A review of research on teaching. In P. Hosford (Ed.), *Using what we know about teaching* (pp. 51–77). ASCD.

Berliner, D. C., & Casanova, U. (1996). *Putting research to work in your school*. Corwin.

Bermudez, C. (2016, May 12). We can't even write a complete sentence and here's why. *Education Post*. http://educationpost.org/we-cant-even-write-a-complete-sentence-and-heres-why

Black, P., & Wiliam, D. (1998, October). Inside the black box. *Phi Delta Kappan*. https://kappanonline.org/inside-the-black-box-raising-standards-through-classroom-assessment

Blanding, M. (2009). Treating the "instructional core": Education rounds. *Usable Knowledge*. www.gse.harvard.edu/news/uk/09/05/treating-instructional-core-education-rounds

Bornstein, D. (2011, April 18). A better way to teach math. *The New York Times*. https://opinionator.blogs.nytimes.com/2011/04/18/a-better-way-to-teach-math

Bracey, G. (2004, December). Value-added assessment findings: Poor kids get poor teachers. *Phi Delta Kappan, 86*(4), 331–333.

Brooks, D. (2022, February 18). The dark century. *The New York Times*. www.nytimes.com/2022/02/17/opinion/liberalism-democracy-russia-ukraine.html

Bryson, M., Maden, A., Mosty, L., & Schultz, S. (2010, October). Doing RTI right. *Educational Leadership, 68*(2). www.ascd.org/publications/educational-leadership/oct10/vol68/num02/Doing-RTI-Right.aspx

Buckingham, M. (2005). *The one thing you need to know*. Free Press.

Burnette II, D. (2018, January 17). What will it take to turn marginal gains into true momentum on school quality? *Education Week*. www.proquest.com/docview/2227387518

Burnton, S. (2012, May 8). 50 stunning Olympic moments No. 28: Dick Fosbury introduces 'the flop.' *The Guardian*. www.theguardian.com/sport/blog/2012/may/08/50-stunning-olympic-moments-dick-fosbury

Calkins, L., Montgomery, K., & Santman, D. (with Faulk, B.). (1998). *A teacher's guide to standardized reading tests: Knowledge is power*. Heinemann.

Carey, K. (2011, November 22). The dissenter. *The New Republic*. https://newrepublic.com/article/97765/diane-ravitch-education-reform

Carmody, T. (2012, January 17). What's wrong with education cannot be fixed with technology: The other Steve Jobs. *Wired*. www.wired.com/2012/01/apple-education-jobs

Carnegie Corporation of New York. (2018, December 11). Parents 2018: Going beyond good grades. *Learning Heroes*. www.carnegie.org/our-work/article/survey-parents-and-teachers-looks-role-report-cards-causing-confusion-over-student-achievement

Chesley, G. M., & Jordan, J. (2012, May). What's missing from teacher prep. *Educational Leadership, 69*(8), 41–45.

Clarfield, M. (2004, March). The Flexner report: One that was not shelved. *Annals of Long-Term Care, 12*(3), 31–32.

Collins, J. (2001). *Good to great.* Harper Business.

Conley, D. (2005). *College knowledge: What it really takes for students to succeed and what we can do to get them ready.* Jossey-Bass.

Conley, D. (2007, April). The challenge of college readiness. *Educational Leadership, 64*(7), 23–29.

Corcoran, T., Fuhrman, S. H., & Belcher, C. L. (2001, September). The district role in instructional improvement. *Phi Delta Kappan, 83*(1), 78–84.

Crossland, J. (2015, March). Is Piaget wrong? *Primary Science, 137,* 30–32. https://eric.ed.gov/?id=EJ1156986

Danielson, C. (2015, April). Framing discussions about teaching. *Educational Leadership, 72*(7), 38–41.

Darling-Hammond. L. (2010). *The flat world of education.* Teachers College Press.

Darling-Hammond, L. (2010–2011, Winter). Soaring systems. *American Educator, 34*(4), 20–23.

Darling-Hammond, L. (2020, May 26). Only a teacher: Interview with Linda Darling-Hammond. *PBS.* www.pbs.org/onlyateacher/today2.html

Delpit, L. (2012). *Multiplication is for white people.* The New Press.

Dewitt, P. (2016, April 19). The myth of walkthroughs: 8 unobserved practices in classrooms. *Education Week.* www.edweek.org/leadership/opinion-the-myth-of-walkthroughs-8-unobserved-practices-in-classrooms/2016/04

Didau, D. (2017). The problems with "zone of proximal development." *Learning Spy Newsletter.* https://learningspy.co.uk/featured/problems-zone-proximal-development

Dillon, S. (2004, December 7). What corporate America can't build: A sentence. *The New York Times.* www.nytimes.com/2004/12/07/business/what-corporate-america-cant-build-a-sentence.html

DuFour, R., DuFour, R., Eaker, R., Many, T. W., & Mattos, M. (2006). *Learning by doing.* Solution Tree.

DuFour, R., & Marzano, R. (2011). *Leaders and learning.* Solution Tree.

Ede, L. (1987). *A sourcebook for basic writing teachers.* Random House.

EdWeek Research Center. (2020, January 21). Early reading instruction: The results of a national survey. www.edweek.org/research-center/research-center-reports/early-reading-instruction-results-of-a-national-survey

Ehrenworth, M. (2017, February 1). Why argue? *Educational Leadership, 74*(5). www.ascd.org/el/articles/why-argue

Elmore, R. (1999–2000, Winter). Building a new structure for school leadership. *American Educator.* https://files.eric.ed.gov/fulltext/ED546618.pdf

Elmore, R. (2005). Building new knowledge: School improvement requires new knowledge, not just good will. *American Educator, 29*(1), 20–27.

Elmore, R. (2006, November/December). Three thousand missing hours. *Harvard Education Letter.* www.hepg.org/hel-home/issues/22_6/helarticle/three-thousand-missing-hours_314

Englemann, S., Haddox, P., & Bruner, E. (1983). *Teach your child to read in 100 easy lessons.* Simon & Schuster.

Ermeling, B., & Graff-Ermeling, G. (2016, November 8). Reframing professional learning. *Teachers College Record.* www.researchgate.net/publication/309980251_Reframing_professional_learning

Ferguson, R. (2016, May). Aiming higher together: Strategizing better educational outcomes for boys and young men of color. Urban Institute. www.urban.org/

sites/default/files/publication/80481/2000784-Aiming-Higher-Together
-Strategizing-Better-Educational-Outcomes-for-Boys-and-Young-Men-of
-Color.pdf

Ferlazzo, L. (2021, July 19). Four good teaching strategies and how to use them. *Education Week.* www.edweek.org/teaching-learning/opinion-four-good-science
-teaching-strategies-how-to-use-them/2021/07

Ferrandino, V. L., & Tirozzi, G. (2004, May 5). Wanted: A comprehensive literacy agenda preK–12. *Education Week, 23*(24), 29.

Field, K. (2021, August 16). Can you fix middle school by getting rid of it? *The Hechinger Report.* https://hechingerreport.org/can-you-fix-middle-school-by
-getting-rid-of-it

Finn, C. E. (2017, April 5). Curriculum becomes a reform strategy. *Flypaper.* https://
fordhaminstitute.org/national/commentary/curriculum-becomes-reform
-strategy

Finn, C. E., & Steiner, D. (2019, February 26). The hidden logic of American underachievement. *Education Week.* www.edweek.org/leadership/opinion-the
-hidden-logic-of-american-underachievement/2019/02

Fisher, D., & Frey, N. (2007). *Checking for understanding.* ASCD.

Foley, D. (2016, August 12). Why grad rates are meaningless. *Intellectual Takeout.*
www.intellectualtakeout.org/blog/why-grad-rates-are-meaningless

Ford, M. P., & Opitz, M. F. (2002, May). Using centers to engage children during guided reading time: Intensifying learning experiences away from the teacher. *The Reading Teacher, 55*(8), 710–717.

Frey, J. (2021, December 16). Civility, democracy, and education. *Flypaper.* https://
fordhaminstitute.org/national/commentary/civility-democracy-and-education

Friedman, T. L. (2005). *The world is flat: A brief history of the 21st century.* Farrar, Straus, and Giroux.

Fullan, M. (2010). *Motion leadership: The skinny on becoming change savvy.* Corwin.

Gallagher, K. (2009). *Readicide: How schools are killing reading and what you can do about it.* Stenhouse.

Gallagher, K. (2017, February). The writing journey. *Educational Leadership, 74*(5), 24–29.

Gamerman, E. (2008, February 29). What makes Finnish kids so smart? *The Wall Street Journal.* www.wsj.com/articles/SB120425355065601997#:~:text=They%20
have%20no%20school%20uniforms,the%20smartest%20in%20the%20world

Gardner, W. (2015, May 4). Credit recovery is a scam. *Education Week.* www.edweek
.org/education/opinion-credit-recovery-is-a-scam/2015/05

Gewertz, C. (2017, August 1). Who gets hurt when high school diplomas are not created equal? *Education Week.* www.edweek.org/teaching-learning/who-gets-hurt
-when-high-school-diplomas-are-not-created-equal/2017/08

Gewertz, C. (2018, February 9). D.C.'s scandal and the nationwide problem of fudging graduation numbers. *Education Week.* www.edweek.org/teaching-learning/d-c-s
-scandal-and-the-nationwide-problem-of-fudging-graduation-numbers/2018/02

Gilbert, E. (2019, November 7). How ed schools became a bastion of bad ideas. *Chronicle of Higher Education.* www.chronicle.com/article/how-ed-schools
-became-a-bastion-of-bad-ideas

Glenn, C. (2018, January 22). School standards in the Bay State. *National Review.* www
.nationalreview.com/magazine/2018/01/22/david-p-driscoll-common-sense-review

Goldberg, M. (2021, June 28). The maddening critical race theory debate. *The New York Times.* www.nytimes.com/2021/06/28/opinion/critical-race-theory.html

Goldstein, M. (2020, January 8). Watch the movie, don't just read the script: Teaching vs. curriculum. *Flypaper*. https://fordhaminstitute.org/national/commentary/watch-movie-dont-just-read-script-teaching-vs-curriculum

Gonzalez, J. (2015, April 29). Protesters eye bogus classes used to boost graduation rates. *New York Daily News*. www.nydailynews.com/new-york/education/gonzalez-protesters-aim-classes-boost-grad-rates-article-1.2202945

Gonzalez, J. (2016, October 30). Is your lesson a Grecian urn? *Cult of Pedagogy*. www.cultofpedagogy.com/grecian-urn-lesson

Gonzalez, J. (2018, March 26). Frickin' packets. *Cult of Pedagogy*. www.cultofpedagogy.com/busysheets

Good, T. L., & Brophy, J. E. (1997). *Looking into classrooms*. Longman.

Goodlad, J. I., et al. (1970). *Behind the classroom door*. Charles A. Jones.

Goodwin, B. (2011). *Simply better: Doing what matters most to change the odds for student success*. ASCD/McRel.

Goodwin, B. (2021, May). Zombie ideas in education. *Educational Leadership, 78*(8). www.ascd.org/el/articles/zombie-ideas-in-education

Graff, G. (2003). *Clueless in academe*. Yale University Press.

Graham, S. (2019, March). Changing how writing is taught. *Review of Research in Education, 43,* 277–303.

Green, E. (2010, March 2). Building a better teacher. *The New York Times Magazine*. www.nytimes.com/2010/03/07/magazine/07Teachers-t.html

Green, E. (2014). *Building a better teacher*. Norton.

Greenberg, J., McKee, A., & Walsh, K. (2013). *Teacher prep review 2013*. National Council on Teacher Quality.

Greenstone, M., Harris, M., Li, K., Looney, A., & Patashnik, J. (2012). A dozen economic facts about K–12 education. *Policy Memo*. www.hamiltonproject.org/assets/legacy/files/downloads_and_links/THP_12EdFacts_2.pdf

Hansen, E. T. (2013, March 11). Top students, too, aren't always ready for college. *Chronicle of Higher Education*. www.chronicle.com/article/top-students-too-arent-always-ready-for-college

Hanson, M. (2022, November 22). College dropout rates. *Education Data Initiative*. https://educationdata.org/college-dropout-rates

Hanushek, E. A. (2018, June 6). What do test scores really mean for the economy? *Education Week*. www.edweek.org/teaching-learning/opinion-what-do-test-scores-really-mean-for-the-economy/2018/06

Harrington, T. (2018, January 4). A focus on writing in every class is key to success in this rural California district. *EdSource*. https://edsource.org/2018/a-focus-on-writing-in-every-class-is-key-to-success-in-this-rural-california-district/592228

Harrington-Lueker, D. (2002, September 16). "Crayola curriculum" takes over. *USA Today*, A–13.

Harris, K., Graham, S., Mason, L., & Friedlander, B. (2008). *Powerful writing strategies for all students*. Brookes.

Harrison, R. (2010, June 23). Board member wants unit 2 schools to "stop wasting time." *Daily News Online*.

Hattie, J. (2009). *Visible learning*. Routledge.

Haycock, K. (2005, June 8). Improving academic achievement and closing gaps between groups in the middle grades. Presentation given at CASE Middle Level Summit. www.edtrust.org.

Heath, C., & Heath D. (2011, March). Overcoming resistance to change. *School Administrator, 68*(3), 28–32.

Hernandez, A., Kaplan, M. A., & Schwartz, R. (2006, October). For the sake of argument. *Educational Leadership, 64*(2), 48–52.

Hernandez, D. J. (2012, January 1). Double jeopardy: How third grade reading skills and poverty influence high school graduation rates. Annie E. Casey Foundation. www.aecf.org/resources/double-jeopardy

Herold, B. (2019, November 5). What is personalized learning? *Education Week.* www.edweek.org/technology/what-is-personalized-learning/2019/11

Hess, F. (2022, January 19). What it means to teach like a champion in 2022. *Education Week.*

Hess, F. M., & Addison, J. G. (2020, December 18). "Anti-racist" education is neither. *The American Mind.* https://americanmind.org/memo/anti-racist-education-is-neither

Hess, R. (2021a). Remembering Harvard's Richard Elmore. *Education Week.* www.edweek.org/policy-politics/opinion-remembering-harvards-richard-elmore/2021/02

Hess, R. (2021b). After all that commotion, was the Common Core a big nothingburger? *Education Week.* www.edweek.org/teaching-learning/opinion-after-all-that-commotion-was-common-core-a-big-nothingburger/2021/04

Hess, R., & Goldstein, M. (2022, January 22). The empty pageantry of education research. *Education Week.* www.edweek.org/leadership/opinion-the-empty-pageantry-of-education-research/2022/01

Hillocks, G. (1987, May). Synthesis of research on teaching writing. *Educational Leadership, 44*(8), 71–82.

Hirsch, E. D. (2010, January 14). First, do no harm. *Education Week, 29*(17), 30–31, 40.

Hirsch, E. D. (2016). *Why knowledge matters.* Harvard Education Press.

Hirsch, E. D. (2020). *How to educate a citizen.* HarperCollins.

Hochman, J., & Wexler, N. (2017). *The writing revolution.* Jossey Bass.

Hopkins, J. R. (2011, December 1). The enduring influence of Jean Piaget. Association for Psychological Science. www.psychologicalscience.org/observer/jean-piaget

HuffPost. (2014, December 12). The U.S. illiteracy rate hasn't changed in 10 years. www.lb7.uscourts.gov/documents/14-3613URL2Illiteracy.pdf

Hurley, P. (2015, Feb 9). Communication named most sought-after skill set in corporate recruiter survey. *Hurley Write blog.* www.hurleywrite.com/blog/Communication-Named-Most-Sought-After-Skill-Set-in-Corporate-Recruiter-Surv

Joyce, B., Wolf, J., & Calhoun, B. (1993). *The self-renewing school.* ASCD.

Kalanithi, P. (2016). *When breath becomes air.* Random House.

Kalenze, E. (2014). *Education is upside down.* Rowman & Littlefield.

Kameenui, E. J., & Carnine, D. W. (1998). *Effective teaching strategies that accommodate diverse learners.* Merrill.

Kane, T. J., & Steiner, D. (2019, April 1). Don't give up on curriculum reform just yet. *Education Week.* www.edweek.org/leadership/opinion-dont-give-up-on-curriculum-reform-just-yet/2019/04

Kessler, A. (2021, November 29). A California attempt to repair the crumbling pillar of education. *The Wall Street Journal.* www.wsj.com/articles/the-crumbling-pillar-of-education-california-dave-welch-vergara-school-choice-charter-11638115242

Killian, S. (2017). Top 10 evidence-based teaching strategies. *UNL Announce.* http://newsroom.unl.edu/announce/csmce/5272/29630

Kirkland, D. (2019, January/February). The truth behind the pipeline. *Literacy Today, 36*(4),10–11.

Kirschner, P., Sweller, J., & Clark, R. E. (2010, June 8). Why minimal guidance during instruction does not work: An analysis of the failure of constructivist, discovery, problem-based, experiential, and inquiry-based teaching. *Educational Psychologist.* www.tandfonline.com/doi/pdf/10.1207/s15326985ep4102_1

Klein, A. (2020, January 21). Flexible seating: Collaboration catalyst or classroom management disaster? *Education Week.* www.edweek.org/teaching-learning/flexible-seating-collaboration-catalyst-or-classroom-disaster/2020/01

Kraft, M., & Gilmour, A. (2017). Revisiting the widget effect: Teacher evaluation reforms and the distribution of teacher effectiveness. *Educational Researcher, 46*(5), 234–249. https://scholar.harvard.edu/mkraft/publications/revisiting-widget-effect-teacher-evaluation-reforms-and-distribution-teacher

Kuhrt, B. L., & Farris, P. J. (1990, March). Empowering students through reading, writing, and reasoning. *Journal of Reading, 33*(6), 436–441.

Landsberg, M. (2008, June 21). Teacher instills a love of words, but the lesson is about life. *Los Angeles Times.* www.latimes.com/local/la-me-holmes21-2008jun21-story.html

Lane, J., & Gustafson, J. (2020, February 12). Training teachers to fail. *Flypaper.* https://fordhaminstitute.org/national/commentary/training-teachers-fail

La Salle, R. A., & Johnson, R. (2019, April). How our language feeds inequity. *Educational Leadership.* www.ascd.org/el/articles/how-our-language-feeds-inequity

Lasch, C. (1995). *Revolt of the elites.* Norton.

Lattier, D. (2016, June 24). Many college students are book virgins. *Intellectual Takeout.* www.intellectualtakeout.org/blog/many-college-students-are-book-virgins

Lee, H. (1960). *To kill a mockingbird.* Grand Central Publishing.

Lemov, D. (2015). *Teach like a champion 2.0.* Jossey-Bass.

Levine, A. (2006, September). Educating schoolteachers. Education Schools Project. https://eric.ed.gov/?id=ED504144

Lipson, M. Y., & Wixson, K. K. (2008, August/September). New IRA commission will address RTI issues. *Reading Today, 26*(1), 1, 5.

Little, J. W., Gearhart, M., Curry, M., & Kafka, J. (2003, November). Looking at student work for teacher learning, teacher community, and school reform. *Phi Delta Kappan, 85*(3), 185–192.

Los Angeles Times. (2021, September 7). Editorial: Learning loss is real. Stop pretending otherwise. www.latimes.com/opinion/story/2021-09-02/editorial-learning-loss-is-real-stop-pretending-otherwise

Loveless, T. (2020, January 14). Common Core has not worked. *Education Next.* www.educationnext.org/common-core-has-not-worked-forum-decade-on-has-common-core-failed

Marino, J. (1988, February). Between the lines of Goodlad, Boyer, and Sizer. *English Journal, 77*(2), 19–21.

Marshall, K. (2003, October). A principal looks back: Standards matter. *Phi Delta Kappan, 85*(2), 105–113.

Marshall, K. (2005, June). It's time to rethink teacher supervision and evaluation. *Phi Delta Kappan, 86*(10), 727–744.

Marshall, K. (2021, April 26). A tribute to Robert Slavin. *Marshall Memo* 884. https://marshallmemo.com/issues/1fc01f2d1b94377b0ffb8ae28f51c85c/MarshMemo884.pdf

Martin, G. R. R. (2011). *A dance with dragons*. Bantam Books.

Marzano, R. J. (2003). *What works in schools: Translating research into action*. ASCD.

Marzano, R. J. (2007). *The art and science of teaching*. ASCD.

Marzano, R. J., Pickering, D. J., & Pollock, J. E. (2001). *Classroom instruction that works*. ASCD.

McGurn, W. (2021, September 6). The real structural racism. *The Wall Street Journal*. www.wsj.com/articles/systemic-structural-racism-naep-report-card-harvard-law-suit-supreme-court-affirmative-action-black-educational-achievement-11630956788

McKibben, S. (2020, September). "Antiracist" grading starts with you. *Educational Leadership*. www.ascd.org/el/articles/turn-and-talk-antiracist-grading-starts-with-you

McWhorter, J. (2021, April 22). No more tests: We should measure black kids on their "desire to know." (St. Ibram, 2019). *It Bears Mentioning*. https://johnmcwhorter.substack.com/p/no-more-tests-we-should-measure-black

Mehta, J., & Fine, S. (2019, March 30). High school doesn't have to be boring. *The New York Times*. www.nytimes.com/2019/03/30/opinion/sunday/fix-high-school-education.html

Miller, M. (2003). *The two percent solution*. Public Affairs.

Mitchell, R. (2004, April 27). Dumbing down our schools. *The Washington Post*, A21. www.washingtonpost.com/archive/opinions/2004/04/27/dumbing-down-our-schools/14608fbf-c002-477a-904e-5f1953eb5d30

Morson, G. S., & Schapiro, M. (2021, September 22). Break the silence. *Persuasion*. www.persuasion.community/p/break-the-silence

Mortimore, P., & Sammons, P. (1987, September). New evidence on effective elementary schools. *Educational Leadership, 45*(1), 4–8.

National Center for Education Statistics. (2020). NAEP reading performance. https://nces.ed.gov/programs/coe/pdf/coe_cnb.pdf

National Commission on Writing. (2003, April). *The neglected "R": The need for a writing revolution*. The College Board.

National Council for Accreditation of Teacher Education. (2010, November). *Transforming teacher education through clinical practice*. www.highered.nysed.gov/pdf/NCATECR.pdf

Newcombe, T. (2015, May 14). What went wrong with L.A. Unified's iPad program? Government Technology. www.govtech.com/education/what-went-wrong-with-la-unifieds-ipad-program.html

Odden, A. (2009, December 9). We know how to turn schools around—we just haven't done it. *Education Week, 29*(14), 22–23.

Odden, A., & Kelley, C. (2002). *Paying teachers for what they know and do*. Corwin.

Olson, L. (1995, February 8). Students' best writing needs work, study shows. *Education Week, 14*(20), 5.

Otterman, S. (2011, July 21). Ed school's pedagogical puzzle. *The New York Times*. www.nytimes.com/2011/07/24/education/edlife/edl-24teacher-t.html

Paulson, A. (2014, November 18). Report: Students read way below level that prepares them for college, careers. *Christian Science Monitor*. www.csmonitor.com/USA/Education/2014/1118/Report-Students-read-way-below-level-that-prepares-them-for-college-careers

Payne, C. (2007). *So much reform, so little change.* Harvard Education Press.

Pearson, P. D., & Gallagher, M. (1983, October). The instruction of reading comprehension. *Contemporary Educational Psychology, 8*(3), 317–344.

Peery, A. (2021, June 14). Does your school need a literacy check-up? *Cult of Pedagogy.* www.cultofpedagogy.com/literacy-check-up

Peters, T., & Waterman, R. H. (1982). *In search of excellence.* Harper & Row.

Petrilli, M. J. (2014, March). *Toward a golden age of educational practice.* Thomas B. Fordham Institute. https://fordhaminstitute.org/national/research/toward -golden-age-educational-practice

Petrilli, M. J. (2015, August 12). The new ESEA will be "loose-loose" because Arne Duncan went overboard with "tight-tight." *Flypaper.* https://edexcellence.net/ articles/the-new-esea-will-be-%E2%80%9Cloose-loose%E2%80%9D -because-arne-duncan-went-overboard-with-%E2%80%9Ctight-tight% E2%80%9D

Petrilli, M. J. (2016, July 6). College readiness versus college completion: Variations by race. *Flypaper.* https://fordhaminstitute.org/national/commentary/college -readiness-versus-college-completion-variations-race

Petrilli, M. J. (2017, Winter). Common confusion. *Education Next.* www.educationnext .org/common-confusion-state-standards-tests-proficiency

Petrilli, M. J. (2018, October 19). Petrilli: From report cards to parent-teacher conferences, schools must do a better job of telling families how their kids are doing. *The74.* www.the74million.org/article/petrilli-from-report-cards-to -parent-teacher-conferences-schools-must-do-a-better-job-of-telling-families -how-their-kids-are-doing

Petrilli, M. J. (2021, October 7). The college gender gap begins in kindergarten. *Flypaper.* https://fordhaminstitute.org/national/commentary/college-gender -gap-begins-kindergarten

Phi Delta Kappan. (2019). *Frustration in the schools.* [Supplemental material] PDK poll of the public's attitudes toward the public schools. *Phi Delta Kappan, 101*(1), K1–K23. https://pdkpoll.org/wp-content/uploads/2020/05/pdkpoll51 -2019.pdf

Pianta, R., Belsky, J., Houts, R., & Morrison, F. (2007, March). Teaching: Opportunities to learn in America's elementary classrooms. *Science, 315*(5820), 1795–1796.

Polikoff, M., & Dean, J. (2019, December 10). The supplemental curriculum bazaar: Is what's online any good? https://fordhaminstitute.org/national/research/ supplemental-curriculum-bazaar

Pondiscio, R. (2014, June 26). Conscious incompetence. *Flypaper.* https://fordham institute.org/national/commentary/conscious-incompetence-new-ed-school -grads-are-unprepared-teach-and-we-seem

Pondiscio, R. (2016, May 16). Failing by design. *Flypaper.* https://fordhaminstitute.org/ national/commentary/failing-design-how-we-make-teaching-too-hard-mere -mortals

Pondiscio, R. (2019, May 15). What we know about early learning. *Flypaper.* https://fordhaminstitute.org/national/commentary/what-we-know-about -early-learning

Pondiscio, R. (2021a, Feb.11). Literacy is equity. *Flypaper.* https://fordhaminstitute .org/national/commentary/literacy-equity

Pondiscio, R. (2021b, April 8). High-quality curriculum doesn't teach itself. *Flypaper.* https://fordhaminstitute.org/national/commentary/high-quality-curriculum -doesnt-teach-itself

Pondiscio, R. (2021c, April 29). I believe "antiracism" is misguided. Can I still teach Black children? *Flypaper.* https://fordhaminstitute.org/national/commentary/i-believe-antiracism-misguided-can-i-still-teach-black-children

Popham, W. J. (2008). *Transformative assessment.* ASCD.

Poplin, M., Rivera, J., Durish, D., Hoff, L., Kawell, S., Pawlak, P., Hinman, I. S., Straus, L., & Veney, C. (2011, February). She's strict for a good reason. *Phi Delta Kappan, 92*(5), 39–43.

Postman, N. (1996). *The end of education.* New York.

Quindlen, A. (2022). *Write for your life.* Random House.

Ravitch, D. (2000). *Left back: A century of failed school reforms.* Simon & Schuster.

Ravitch, D. (2011, May 31). Waiting for a school miracle. *The New York Times.* www.nytimes.com/2011/06/01/opinion/01ravitch.html

Rea, A. (2020, April 26). How serious is America's literacy problem? *The Library Journal.* www.libraryjournal.com/story/How-Serious-Is-Americas-Literacy-Problem

Reeves, D. B. (2007, November). Leading to change/How do you sustain excellence? *Educational Leadership, 65*(30), 86–87.

Reznitskaya, A., & Wilkinson, I. (2019, May 7). Teaching students how to think and argue together. *Voices in Education.* www.hepg.org/blog/teaching-students-how-to-think-and-argue-together

Richtel, M. (2011, September 3). In classroom of future, stagnant scores. *The New York Times.* www.nytimes.com/2011/09/04/technology/technology-in-schools-faces-questions-on-value.html

Riley, B. (2017, March). Personalization vs. how people learn. *Educational Leadership, 74*(6), 68–72.

Riley, N. S. (2018, August 14). *How Schools Work* review: The worm in the apple. *The Wall Street Journal.* www.wsj.com/articles/how-schools-work-review-the-worm-in-the-apple-1534201715

Riley, N. S. (2020a). Bad teaching is tearing America apart. Interview with E. D. Hirsch. *The Wall Street Journal.* www.wsj.com/articles/bad-teaching-is-tearing-america-apart-11599857351

Riley, N. S. (2020b). My kids and their elite education in racism. *Commentary.* www.commentary.org/articles/naomi-schaefer-riley/elite-education-racism

Ripley, A. (2013). *The smartest kids in the world.* Simon & Schuster.

Rose, M. (1989). *Lives on the boundary.* Viking Penguin.

Rosenholtz, S. J. (1991). *Teachers' workplace: The social organization of schools.* Teachers College Press.

Rosenshine, B. (2012, Spring). Principles of instruction: Research-based strategies that all teachers should know. *American Educator, 36*(1), 12–19, 39.

Russakoff, D. (2015). *The prize.* Houghton Mifflin Harcourt.

Sahm, C. (2017, January 10). Why curriculum counts. *Flypaper.* https://edexcellence.net/articles/why-curriculum-counts

Samuels, A. (2022, February 24). A principal explains how to repair the harm of "college for all." *Flypaper.* https://fordhaminstitute.org/national/commentary/principal-explains-how-repair-harm-college-all

Sanders, W. L., & Horn, S. P. (1994, October). The Tennessee value-added assessment system. *Journal of Personnel Evaluation Education, 8*(3), 299–311.

Sawchuk, S. (2013, July 9). Disputed review finds disparities in teacher prep. *Education Week.* www.edweek.org/leadership/disputed-review-finds-disparities-in-teacher-prep/2013/07

Sawchuk, S., & Schwartz, S. (2019, July 18). Influential reading group makes it clear: Students need systematic, explicit phonics. *Education Week*. www.edweek.org/teaching-learning/influential-reading-group-makes-it-clear-students-need-systematic-explicit-phonics/2019/07

Schaffer, R. H. (1988). *The breakthrough strategy*. Harper Business.

Schaffhauser, D. (2017, March 13). Short-term impact of $3 billion school improvement grants: Zilch. *THE Journal*. https://thejournal.com/articles/2017/03/13/short-term-impact-of-3-billion-school-improvement-grants-zilch.aspx

Schmidt, M. (2020, August 28). How reading fiction increases empathy and encourages understanding. *Discover Magazine*. www.discovermagazine.com/mind/how-reading-fiction-increases-empathy-and-encourages-understanding

Schmoker, M. (1999). *Results: The key to continuous school improvement*. ASCD.

Schmoker, M. (2001, October 24). The Crayola curriculum. *Education Week, 21*(8), 42–44.

Schmoker, M. (2006). *Results now*. ASCD.

Schmoker, M. (2018). *Focus: Elevating the essentials to radically improve student learning* (2nd ed.). ASCD.

Schmoker, M. (2019a). How to make reading instruction much, much, much more efficient. *Education Week*. www.edweek.org/teaching-learning/opinion-how-to-make-reading-instruction-much-much-more-efficient/2019/11

Schmoker, M. (2019b). The problem with literacy programs. *Education Week*. www.edweek.org/teaching-learning/opinion-the-problem-with-literacy-programs/2019/02

Schmoker, M. (2019c, September). Focusing on the essentials. *Educational Leadership*. www.ascd.org/el/articles/focusing-on-the-essentials

Schmoker, M. (2020, February). Radical reset: The case for minimalist literacy standards. *Educational Leadership*. www.ascd.org/el/articles/radical-reset-the-case-for-minimalist-literacy-standards

Schmoker, M. (2022, June 3). No, fewer books, less writing won't add up to media literacy. *Education Week*. www.edweek.org/teaching-learning/opinion-no-fewer-books-less-writing-wont-add-up-to-media-literacy/2022/06

Schmoker, M. (n.d.). Write more, grade less. *Mike Schmoker*. mikeschmoker.com/write-more.html

Schmoker, M., & Marzano, R. (1999). Realizing the promise of standards-based education. *Educational Leadership, 56*(6), 17–21.

Schwartz, S. (2019, December 3). The most popular reading programs aren't backed by science. *Education Week*. www.edweek.org/teaching-learning/the-most-popular-reading-programs-arent-backed-by-science/2019/12

Schwartz, S. (2021, June 22). Algebra 1 is a turning point. Here's how to help incoming students: A case study on getting kids ready for the gatekeeper math course. *Education Week*. www.edweek.org/teaching-learning/algebra-1-is-a-turning-point-heres-how-to-help-incoming-students/2021/06

Second-Year Teacher/Anonymous. (2008, Spring). There's a hole in state standards. *American Educator*. www.aft.org/periodical/american-educator/spring-2008/theres-hole-state-standards

Seidenberg, M. (2017). *Language at the speed of sight*. BasicBooks.

Sewall, G. T. (2000, Summer). Lost in action. *American Educator*. www.aft.org/periodical/american-educator/summer-2000/lost-action

Shanahan, T. (2014, September 26). How and how not to prepare students for the new tests. *The Reading Teacher, 68*(3), 184–188. www.scribd.com/document/265954704 /How-and-How-Not-to-Prepare-Students-for-the-New-Tests-Shanahan-T

Shanahan, T. (2018, October 13). *Shanahan on literacy.* www.shanahanonliteracy.com/ blog/do-learning-centers-and-seatwork-improve-reading-achievement#sthash .rB3ebugi.dpbs

Shanahan, T., & Shanahan, C. (2017, February). Disciplinary literacy: Just the FAQs. *Educational Leadership, 74*(5), 18–22.

Singal, D. J. (1991, November). The other crisis in American education. *The Atlantic Monthly, 268*(5), 59–74.

Slavin, R. (2019, May 16). Can computers teach? https://robertslavinsblog.wordpress .com/2019/05/16/can-computers-teach

Slavin, R., Lake, C., Inns, A., Baye, A., Dachet, D., & Haslam, J. (2019, July). Writing approaches in years 3 to 13: Evidence review. *Education Endowment Foundation.* https://educationendowmentfoundation.org.uk/public/files/Writing_Approaches_ in_Years_3_to_13_Evidence_Review.pdf

Sonbert, M. (2019, November 20). Biggest trend in teaching today. *Education Week.* www.edweek.org/education/opinion-the-biggest-trend-in-teaching-today/ 2019/11

Sparks, S. D. (2011, February 28). Experts say RTI's use may outrun its research base. *Education Week.* www.edweek.org/teaching-learning/experts-say-rtis-use-may -outrun-its-research-base/2011/02

Sparks, S. D. (2015, November 11). RTI practice falls short of promise, research finds. *Education Week, 35*(12).

Sparks, S. D. (2017, January 19). Billions in school improvement spending but not much student improvement. *Education Week.* www.edweek.org/leadership/billions-in -school-improvement-spending-but-not-much-student-improvement/2017/01

Sparks, S. D. (2018, August 26). Are classroom reading groups the best way to teach reading? Maybe not. *Education Week.* www.edweek.org/teaching-learning/are -classroom-reading-groups-the-best-way-to-teach-reading-maybe-not/2018/08

Sparks, S. D. (2020a, February 12). In many districts, a child's academic trajectory is set by 3rd grade. *Education Week.* www.edweek.org/leadership/in-many-districts-a -childs-academic-trajectory-is-set-by-3rd-grade/2020/02

Sparks, S. D. (2020b, October 28). Even before pandemic, national test finds most seniors unready for college reading, math. *Education Week.* www.edweek.org/ teaching-learning/even-before-pandemic-national-test-finds-most-seniors -unready-for-college-reading-math/2020/10

Sparks, S. D. (2021, June 15). Is the bottom falling out for readers who struggle the most? *Education Week.* www.edweek.org/teaching-learning/is-the-bottom -falling-out-for-readers-who-struggle-the-most/2021/06

Sparks, S. (2022, March 2). Classroom reading groups: 5 lessons from recent studies. *Education Week.* www.edweek.org/teaching-learning/classroom-reading-groups -5-lessons-from-recent-studies/2022/03

Sparks, R. L, Patton, J. A., & Murdoch, A. (2013, March 31). Early reading success and its relationship to reading achievement and reading volume: Replication of "10 years later." *Reading and Writing, 27*, 189–211.. www.msj.edu/academics/ graduate-programs/teacher-advancement-and-endorsement-programs/reading -science/Sparks,-Patterson,-Murdoch-2014.pdf

Stecher, B. M., et al. (2018). *Improving teacher effectiveness: Final report*. RAND.

Steiner, D. (2017, August 21). Choosing a curriculum: A critical act. *Education Next*. www.educationnext.org/choosing-curriculum-critical-act

Stern, S. (2009, Autumn). E. D. Hirsch's curriculum for democracy. *City Journal*. www .city-journal.org/html/e-d-hirsch%E2%80%99s-curriculum-democracy-13234.html

Stevens, K. B. (2015, May 4). Early-education teachers need better training. *Education Week*. www.edweek.org/teaching-learning/opinion-early-education-teachers -need-better-training/2015/05?cmp=ENL-EU-NEWS2

Stoltzfus, K. (2017, April 19). Joyful schools: What one U.S. educator learned from teaching in Finland. *Education Week Teacher*. http://blogs.edweek.org/teachers/ teaching_now/2017/04/joyful_schools_what_one_us_educator_learned_from _teaching_in_finland.html

Stotsky, S. (1999). *Losing our language: How multicultural classroom instruction is undermining our children's ability to read, write, and reason*. Free Press.

Strauss, V. (2011, June 30). The trouble with professional development for teachers. *The Washington Post*. www.washingtonpost.com/blogs/answer-sheet/post/the -trouble-with-professional-development-for-teachers/2011/06/30/AGRxQfrH_ blog.html

Strauss, V. (2014a). Why most professional development for teachers is useless. *The Washington Post*. www.washingtonpost.com/news/answer-sheet/ wp/2014/03/01/why-most-professional-development-for-teachers-is-useless

Strauss, V. (2014b). The huge problems with professional development for teachers. *The Washington Post*. www.washingtonpost.com/news/answer-sheet/ wp/2014/09/06/the-huge-problem-with-professional-development-for-teachers

Superville, D. R. (2021, February 16). Top-tier principals spark big gains in student learning. *Education Week*. www.edweek.org/leadership/top-tier-principals-spark -big-gains-in-student-learning-a-new-study-shows-how-much/2021/02

Surowiecki, J. (2014, November 3). Better all the time: How the "performance revolution" came to athletics—and beyond. *The New Yorker*. www.newyorker .com/magazine/2014/11/10/better-time

Tate, E. (2021, March 22). How much does the U.S. spend on edtech? No one knows, and that's a problem. *EdSurge*. www.edsurge.com/news/2021-03-22-how-much -does-the-u-s-spend-on-edtech-no-one-knows-and-that-s-a-problem

Terada, Y., & Merrill, S. (2020, December 4). The 10 most significant education studies of 2020. *Edutopia*. www.edutopia.org/article/10-most-significant-education -studies-2020

The New Teacher Project. (2015, August 4). *The mirage: Confronting the hard truth about our quest for teacher development*. https://tntp.org/publications/view/the -mirage-confronting-the-truth-about-our-quest-for-teacher-development

The New Teacher Project. (2018, September 25). *The opportunity myth*. https://tntp .org/publications/view/the-opportunity-myth

Tierney, J. (2013, April 25). The coming revolution in education. *The Atlantic*. www.theatlantic.com/national/archive/2013/04/the-coming-revolution-in -public-education/275163

Tucker, M. (2015, April 23). Why have American education standards collapsed? *Education Week*. www.edweek.org/teaching-learning/opinion-why-have -american-education-standards-collapsed/2015/04

Tucker, M. (2018, November 1). Teachers colleges: The weakest link. *Education Week*. www.edweek.org/teaching-learning/opinion-teachers-colleges-the-weakest -link/2018/11

Tucker, M. (2021, May 13). Why other countries keep outperforming us in education (and how to catch up). *Education Week.* www.edweek.org/policy-politics/opinion-why-other-countries-keep-outperforming-us-in-education-and-how-to-catch-up/2021/05

Tyre, P. (2012, October). The writing revolution. *The Atlantic.* www.theatlantic.com/magazine/archive/2012/10/the-writing-revolution/309090

Vail, K. (2001, January). Nurturing the life of the mind. *American School Board Journal, 188*(1), 19–23.

Vanderheyden, A., Burns, M., Bron, R., & Tilley, D. (2016). RTI works (when it is implemented correctly). *Education Week, 35*(15), 25.

Varlas, L. (2016, July). Syllabust-ed: Preparing students for the rigors of college reading. *Education Update, 58*(7).

Vlasova, H. (2022, January 7). Eye-opening college dropout rates and statistics. *Admissionsly.* https://admissionsly.com/college-dropout-rates

Wagner, T. (2004, October 27). The challenge of change leadership. *Education Week, 24*(9), 40–41.

Wagner, T. (2008, November 12). Teaching and testing the skills that matter most. *Education Week, 28*(12), 30.

Wahleithner, J. M. (2020, July/August). The high school-college disconnect: Examining first-generation college students' perceptions of their literacy preparation. *Journal of Adolescent and Adult Literacy, 64*(1), 19–26.

Walshe, R. D. (1987, October). The learning power of writing. *English Journal, 76*(6), 22–27.

Ward, A. (2017, May/June). Three components to reading success. *Literacy Today, 34*(6), 10–11.

Wexler, N. (2019). *The knowledge gap.* Avery.

Wexler, N. (2020a). Do the benefits of digital devices in school classrooms outweigh the downsides? *The Wall Street Journal.* www.wsj.com/articles/do-the-benefits-of-digital-devices-in-school-classrooms-outweigh-the-downsides-11582297138

Wexler, N. (2020b). Why kids know even less about history now—and why it matters. *Forbes.* www.forbes.com/sites/nataliewexler/2020/04/24/why-kids-know-even-less-about-history-now-and-why-it-matters

Wiener, R., & Pimentel, S. (2017, April). Practice what you teach. *The Aspen Institute.* https://edexcellence.net/articles/practice-what-you-teach

Wiliam, D. (2007). Content then process: Teacher learning communities in the service of formative assessment. In D. Reeves (Ed.), *Ahead of the curve: The power of assessment to transform teaching and learning* (pp. 182–204). Solution Tree.

Will, M. (2019, February 20). Higher pay leads to smarter teachers, global study says. *Education Week.* www.edweek.org/teaching-learning/higher-pay-leads-to-smarter-teachers-global-study-says/2019/02

Will, M. (2020, February 4). When teachers are tough graders, students learn more. *Education Week.* www.edweek.org/teaching-learning/when-teachers-are-tough-graders-students-learn-more-study-says/2020/02

Will, M. (2021, November 29). Efforts to toughen teacher evaluations show no positive impact on students. *Education Week.* www.edweek.org/teaching-learning/efforts-to-toughen-teacher-evaluations-show-no-positive-impact-on-students/2021/11

Willingham, D. T. (2018, October 29). Just how polarized are we about reading instruction? *Daniel Willingham—Science and Education.* www.danielwillingham

.com/daniel-willingham-science-and-education-blog/just-how-polarized-are-we
-about-reading-instruction

Willingham, D. T. (2019, Summer). Ask the cognitive scientist: Should teachers know the basic science of how children learn? *American Educator, 43*(2), 30–36.

Willingham, D. T., & Rotherham, A. J. (2020, May). Education's research problem. *Educational Leadership, 77*(8), 70–75.

Wineburg, S. (2013, December 10). Using history to invigorate common core lessons. *Education Week.* www.edweek.org/teaching-learning/opinion-using-history-to -invigorate-common-core-lessons/2013/12

Wolfe, T. (1987). *Bonfire of the vanities.* Farrar, Strauss, Giroux.

Wright, B. L. (2018, February 14). *America's graduation rate malfeasance is a symptom of a broken system.* Thomas B. Fordham Institute. https://fordhaminstitute.org/ national/commentary/americas-graduation-rate-malfeasance-symptom-broken -system

Wu, J. (2010, June 10). Grade 3 students lagging on reading. *Boston.com.* http://archive .boston.com/news/education/k_12/mcas/articles/2010/06/10/grade_3_students _lagging_on_reading

Yeh, C. (2017, April 14). Forget grit. Focus on inequality. *Education Week.* www.edweek .org/leadership/opinion-forget-grit-focus-on-inequality/2017/04

Zinsser, W. K. (1988). *Writing to learn.* Harper & Row.

Index

About the Author

Dr. Mike Schmoker is a former administrator, English teacher, and football coach. He has written several bestselling books and dozens of articles for educational journals, newspapers, and *TIME* magazine. His most recent book is the expanded 2018 edition of *FOCUS: Elevating the Essentials to Radically Improve Student Learning*. His previous bestseller, *Results NOW*, was a book of the year finalist by the Association of Education Publishers.

In a 2018 *Education Week* survey of national school leaders, he was ranked among the best sources of "practical advice, wisdom, and insight" on effective school improvement. He is the recipient of the Distinguished Service Award by the National Association of Secondary School Principals for his publications and presentations.

Dr. Schmoker has consulted and keynoted throughout the United States, Canada, Australia, China, and Jordan. He now lives in Tempe, Arizona, with his wife Cheryl.

Related ASCD Resources: School Improvement

At the time of publication, the following resources were available (ASCD stock numbers in parentheses).

The Art and Science of Teaching: A Comprehensive Framework for Effective Instruction by Robert J. Marzano (#107001)

The Artisan Teaching Model for Instructional Leadership: Working Together to Transform Your School by Kenneth Baum & David Krulwich (#116041)

Committing to the Culture: How Leaders Can Create and Sustain Positive Schools by Steve Gruenert & Todd Whitaker (#119007)

Focus: Elevating the Essentials to Radically Improve Student Learning, 2nd Edition by Mike Schmoker (#118044)

Leading with Focus: Elevating the Essentials for School and District Improvement by Mike Schmoker (#116024)

The Learning Leader: How to Focus School Improvement for Better Results, 2nd Edition by Douglas B. Reeves (#118003)

Research-Based Instructional Strategies That Work (Quick Reference Guide) by Bryan Goodwin & Kristin Rouleau (#QRG122037)

Results: The Key to Continuous School Improvement, 2nd Edition by Mike Schmoker (#199233)

The Results Fieldbook: Practical Strategies from Dramatically Improved Schools by Mike Schmoker (#101001)

Understanding Your Instructional Power: Curriculum and Language Decisions to Support Each Student by Tanji Reed Marshall (#122027)

For up-to-date information about ASCD resources, go to www.ascd.org. You can search the complete archives of *Educational Leadership* at www.ascd.org/el.

ASCD myTeachSource®

Download resources from a professional learning platform with hundreds of research-based best practices and tools for your classroom at http://myteachsource.ascd.org/

For more information, send an email to member@ascd.org; call 1-800-933-2723 or 703-578-9600; send a fax to 703-575-5400; or write to Information Services, ASCD, 2800 Shirlington Rd., Suite 1001, Arlington, VA 22206 USA.

ascd
whole child

The ASCD Whole Child approach is an effort to transition from a focus on narrowly defined academic achievement to one that promotes the long-term development and success of all children. Through this approach, ASCD supports educators, families, community members, and policymakers as they move from a vision about educating the whole child to sustainable, collaborative actions.

Results Now 2.0 relates to the **engaged** and **supported** tenets. *For more about the ASCD Whole Child approach, visit* **www.ascd.org/ wholechild.**

WHOLE CHILD
TENETS

1 **HEALTHY**
Each student enters school healthy and learns about and practices a healthy lifestyle.

2 **SAFE**
Each student learns in an environment that is physically and emotionally safe for students and adults.

3 **ENGAGED**
Each student is actively engaged in learning and is connected to the school and broader community.

4 **SUPPORTED**
Each student has access to personalized learning and is supported by qualified, caring adults.

5 **CHALLENGED**
Each student is challenged academically and prepared for success in college or further study and for employment and participation in a global environment.